INSIDE THE INFERNO

A FIREFIGHTER'S STORY OF THE BROTHERHOOD THAT SAVED FORT McMURRAY

DAMIAN ASHER

with OMAR MOUALLEM

Published By Simon & Schuster

NEW YORK   LONDON   TORONTO   SYDNEY   NEW DELHI

SIMON &
SCHUSTER
CANADA

Simon & Schuster Canada
A Division of Simon & Schuster, Inc.
166 King Street East, Suite 300
Toronto, Ontario M5A 1J3

This Simon & Schuster Canada edition April 2017

SIMON & SCHUSTER CANADA and colophon are registered trademarks
of Simon & Schuster, Inc.

For information about special discounts for bulk purchases,
please contact Simon & Schuster Special Sales at 1-800-268-3216
or CustomerService@simonandschuster.ca.

Asher, Damian, author
   Inside the inferno : a firefighter's story of the brotherhood that saved Fort McMurray /
Damian Asher, Omar Mouallem.
Issued in print and electronic formats.
ISBN 978-1-5011-7112-3 (hardcover)—ISBN 978-1-5011-7114-7 (HTML)

   1. Asher, Damian.   2. Wildfires—Alberta—Fort McMurray.   3. Firefighters—
Alberta—Fort McMurray.   4. Fort McMurray (Alta.)—History—21st century.
I. Mouallem, Omar, 1985–, author   II. Title.

SD421.34.C3A84 2017   363.3'90971232   C2017-901255-X
                                                                   C2017-901256-8

Manufactured in the United States of America
10 9 8 7 6 5 4 3 2 1
ISBN 978-1-5011-7112-3
ISBN 978-1-5011-7114-7 (ebook)

Photograph on pages 6–7 courtesy of MagMos/Shutterstock.
Photograph on page 38 courtesy of Captain Damian Asher.
Photographs on pages 50–51 and 134–35 courtesy of Captain Adam Bugden.
Photograph on page 188 courtesy of Chris Relph.

Damian Asher dedicates this book to all the children,
wives, husbands, brothers, sisters, mothers and fathers
of the members of the Fort McMurray Fire Department,
as well as the members of the departments that came to our aid.
A department is a family, and without your support,
no member would have been able to do
what they did in this historic event.
It's a dedication to you members who have moved
to Fort McMurray for a job and have made it a home,
to your support in our community and to your choice
to protect it by laying your lives on the line.
I am humbled to be in your presence and to call you family.

Omar Mouallem dedicates this to his parents, Ahmed and Tamam.

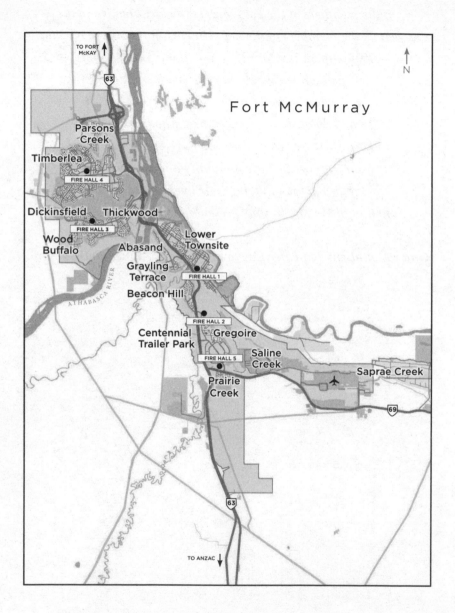

CONTENTS

AUTHORS' NOTE

This book is a narrative construction derived from Damian Asher's telling of the Fort McMurray fires, as well as some twenty interviews of firefighters, locals and wildfire experts. Innumerable weather and government reports, news articles and event timelines were studied to find the most consistent evidence of the truth; however, the authors have taken some creative liberties.

While most characters are based on real people and are depicted using their real names, a few names have been changed, and some characters are composites. The authors have re-drawn conversations and story dialogue, in most cases based on the recollections of those involved. Some public figures appear who were instrumental to true events. In earlier chapters of the book, some scenes were composed to dramatize an average day at the fire hall and to introduce characters to the longer story. These decisions were made thoughtfully and with both the subjects and readers in mind.

PROLOGUE

There's one road in and one road out of Fort McMurray, and that one road was gridlocked. The whole southern lane crowded with cars too slow to outpace clouds of smoke chasing them from the north. The sky, hardly visible through the smoke, was a sea of flames three hundred feet tall in the boreal forest surrounding my city. My city that had turned black and orange in an instant. My city on fire.

Ten minutes ago, I'd arrived at Fire Hall 5 on my afternoon off. When I was called in, the town was hazy but visible and the highway lightly trafficked. By the time I'd buttoned my shirt, laced my duty boots and packed my bunker gear as a precaution, the winds had quickened to sixty kilometres per hour and shifted northeast towards us. I was racing out in a fire engine before the bay door touched the rafters, driving alone into the inferno.

Turning onto the highway with sirens blaring, I dodged cars trying to evacuate from the city. They were climbing from the ditches, barrelling across parking lots and jumping curbs as flakes of burning ember rained on them. The way out of town was bumper-to-bumper and side-door-to-side-door, five lanes of vehicles on a three-lane road, and the northbound route was filling with southbound traffic too. I crushed the air-horn button and swerved into the centre lane, sharing a millisecond of eye contact with the drivers I passed, enough for me to see the fear in their eyes. And now I'd find out for myself what it was they had seen.

The radio hissed. "Captain Asher, it's Training Officer Kratochvil."

"Yeah, go," I snapped back.

"I saw you leaving the hall. I've got the new recruits. We're following you in." A white Ford F-150 swerved behind me, the bed filled with a crew of kneeling firefighters holding on for their lives. "Where are we going?"

"Beacon Hill." That's where my kids go to school. The radio hissed with other chatter, other neighbourhoods under threat, but everything—reports, sirens, honking, the world—it all muted as I imagined Taya and Aidan's classrooms filling with smoke.

My wife and I had received the email from their elementary school, asking for parents to evacuate the students. She'd have to come from the grocery store downtown, but judging from the surrounding mayhem, any town road would be equally gridlocked. The lineup for fuel at gas stations flanking the highway snaked onto arterial streets; the Flying J gas station had no lineup because it was on fire. Roadside onlookers stood in harm's way, gobsmacked by flames on the filling station's roof, flames in the grass, flames across the western horizon. Trees lit up ten at a time as an inferno crested down the valley, carrying flames tall as cellphone towers searing in the hills. Cars scraped each other and people ran up and down the sides of the roads. It wasn't just people in a panic—deer pushed out of the bush by the heat were galloping into town, nearly causing road accidents.

"Melanie! Mel!" I shouted into my cellphone. Her voice was too faint to hear above the sirens, horns and roaring winds. "Did you get them?"

She said something about a traffic jam at Save-On-Foods.

"The fire's hit Beacon Hill. Call Pam! Call Pam!" Pam is our neighbour and the school librarian. She could bring them home.

"I tried, I tried, I tried." Melanie repeated it enough times that I heard it clearly. I told her I loved her and tossed the phone on the passenger seat.

As I approached the intersection of Beacon Hill Drive—the neighbourhood's single entry and exit point, like Highway 63—it was utter chaos. Police officers directing traffic in respirator masks were trying to keep control and move vehicles out. My air horn cleared a narrow path for me to cut through the traffic and enter Beacon Hill. The crew tried to follow my tracks but couldn't keep up. In the haze, I had no clue where I was going until I spotted a school-zone sign.

Good Shepherd School is across from the hill bank, and far from the Hangingstone River, where the wildfire was thought to be contained. But the blaze had done the impossible and jumped two rivers, climbed up the valley and crawled a hundred metres from the only road protecting the children. I braked by the main doors, in the school bus lane. The playgrounds and soccer fields were quiet. The parking lot was empty. It was Tuesday afternoon, but it looked like a Sunday, so I left.

The smoke had thickened, but blew away from me for a clearer sightline. It was brown from the spruce and poplar engulfed by the blaze. I prayed it didn't go black, a chemical reaction from burning synthetics, which could only mean that the fire had touched homes.

Friends' homes. Family's homes. Homes I grew up in. Homes I built with my own two hands as a contractor in my spare time.

As flaming debris and branches blew across the windshield, I stopped myself from thinking of my house on the other side of town, a palatial bungalow I'd spent three years on, hammering every nail and loading every beam. We'd moved in a year ago, and just that morning I'd finally started landscaping. My stomach turned, but I had to focus on the job in front me.

Choppers and tankers whirred over the block of mid-century bungalows around me. They were unscathed, for now, but flames at the greenbelt on the edge of the valley crowned in the spruces, burning their canopies off like dandelion heads. They dropped to earth before torching the trunks. All down the block, residents stuffed their vehicles with bags, pet kennels and kids. Husbands and wives bumped into each other while they bolted in and out of their houses with whatever they could think of, forgetting whatever they'd soon regret.

I parked by a red hydrant near where the fire was crowing out of the trees and heading towards the houses. I flicked the switch for the monitor, and the deluge gun attached to the roof showered the trees. There were 2,000 litres in the tank, but with 4,800 litres sprayed per minute that wouldn't get me far. I radioed dispatch: "Dispatch, this is Captain Asher."

> Sweat dripped on my sleeves. My eyes stung. I coughed into my arm and shielded my face from the unbearable heat.

"Captain Asher, go for dispatch," she responded.

"Dispatch, Captain Asher. I'm on Pumper 310, all by myself, on the corner of Beacon Hill Drive and Beaver Hill Crescent, setting up for fire attack."

"Captain Asher, dispatch. Acknowledge."

I jumped to the pavement and sprinted to the back cabinet for a large inlet hose that was pre-plugged into the truck's tank for a fast connection. Wrench in hand, I hoisted it over my shoulder and pulled it to the hydrant through a blizzard of embers and burning spruce needles. I popped off the steamer port, connected it and turned the nut atop the hydrant. It takes sixteen rotations to open the valve.

One, two, three . . .

Sweat dripped on my sleeves. My eyes stung. I coughed into my arm and shielded my face from the unbearable heat.

Seven, eight, nine . . .

The only sound was windswept flames, roaring like a rolling train that drowned out the sirens and yelling.

Twelve, thirteen, fourteen . . .

Just then, an ember the size of a softball hurtled across the road and smashed through a front window. Flames swallowed the curtains, and with a last twist of the wrench, I watched black smoke engulf the living room.

PART ONE
BEFORE THE BLAZE

CHAPTER 1

LIKE ANY OTHER MONDAY

S oon as my eyes open, I'm awake. Ready to go. Hit the alarm, kiss the wife, grab my bag and slip out the door. I grew into this habit when my kids were newborns, so I didn't disturb them. But it's also my firefighter instinct. You could be deep asleep in dorms, but the instant dispatch calls, lights flash and tones ring, you better get in your gear, out the bay and to the scene in seven minutes. And you better be ready for anything: a house fire, a motor vehicle accident, an overdose, a child birth, or a cardiac arrest. Just look at what's in front of you and get the job done.

Monday, May 2, 2016, the day before the biggest evacuation in Canadian history and the costliest natural disaster this country's ever known, started like any other. That the dawn air stunk of campfire was no more concerning than the plumes in the sky west of me. When you're born and raised in the boreal forest, the lungs of Canada, the scent of burning wood is akin to fermented grapes to a wino. My nostrils took a long, sweet drag of it, tilting skywards at a roaring commercial airliner swooping so low I could read its registration number on the wing. I tossed my gear in the back of my 1999 Toyota Tacoma, a four-seater that's had better days, and set out to Fire Hall 5.

Sunrise gave the smoke columns psychedelic shades, resembling cotton candy in a hazy sky. Ahead of me, two airplane tankers water-bombed the fire with a red retardant blending into the plume, and forestry helicopters circled the periphery. By my estimation it was ten clicks from town, blowing southwest, away from the houses, oil plants and industrial camps. The night before, the wife's friends fussed about the fire on Facebook, but the reality was no big deal. Blazing black spruce has a way of thumping its chest like this, lifting high and fluffing up like a menacing thunderstorm cloud. Besides, forest fires are as much a part of our lives as hunting, fishing and hiking. Or, if you're parents of active kids like Melanie and me, as much a part of life as shuttling from dance recitals to birthday parties.

> Sunrise gave the smoke columns psychedelic shades, resembling cotton candy in a hazy sky.

Not what you think of when you think of Fort McMurray? Doesn't surprise me.

Since the oil boom of the early 2000s, a bunch of foreign reporters have parachuted in and told different versions of the same one-sided story. It's practically a colour-by-numbers picture: shade in the big trucks and six-figure manual labour jobs, the get-rich-quick with no education. Paint in deforestation and pollution. Colour in the poisoned ducks and don't forget to scrawl the idiotic nickname "Fort Mc-Money" on it.

That story might make a good stereotype, but it misses the real draw of our community. Driving to town from Saprae Creek Estates, a woodsy southeast hamlet, I'm reminded of it every day.

On Airport Road, my truck curled around the valley cradling the lower townsite, past the creeks and rivers where Dad taught me to fish, before gliding into the shade of timbered hills flush with spruce, poplar and knotted pine. When I was a child, my family and I would hunt deer and moose in those hills. The Ashers have always been outdoorsy folks, and to this day there's nothing my eight-year-old boy, Aidan, and seven-year-old girl, Taya, love more than quadding the bumpy trails right outside our front door. There are those who see Fort McMurray as nothing more than a place to work—get in, get what you need out of it and leave (and those people always bring their broke asses back for another withdrawal). But the reason third-generation families like mine call it home isn't a mystery.

Nine thousand years ago, a catastrophic flood tore across the continent, carving river valleys, cliffs, coves and inlets into this northern chunk of the Prairies. Another great flood from the Clearwater and Athabasca rivers flattened the centre, forming a perfect habitat for ancient nomads and modern nomads today, representing seventy-six countries. So although Wood Buffalo (the municipality including Fort McMurray, Saprae Creek and the other hamlets) is a dot higher on the map than the capital of Siberia, nature, at its most violent, has sculpted it into something beautiful.

Nature did another amazing thing. It shoved a sticky mixture of gravel and bitumen from the earth's depths to the surface. We now call this pungent tar the oil sands. Ancient people burned it for mosquito repellent and plastered it over their canoe cracks. For centuries after, European settlers couldn't figure out what to do with it. Not until the 1960s did they understand its potential. Suncor led the way, but now a hundred companies make good on this trillion-dollar goop, and the town has seen a steady stream of migrants ever since.

The year my dad was born, 1951, about nine hundred people resided in Fort McMurray's humble trailers and shacks. By the time he and Mom joined the surge of oil and gas prospectors in Alberta twenty-six years later, it was sixteen thousand. Like so many young couples, my parents had been summoned to the promised land, from northern British Columbia, with rumours of big labour shortages and high wages. They followed friends to Fort McMurray one summer, and the first two companies where they applied hired them on sight. Mom had just finished high school and waitressed at a diner popular among oil field workers; their tips overflowed from her apron pocket every shift. Dad was a house-painter, toiling for gigs in B.C. that had become less and less frequent. Up here, he worked overtime as a natural gas lineman every day.

The city continued to grow in the following years, and at last count the population of Wood Buffalo was over 125,000. That includes the "shadow population"—folks in industrial camps, flying in and flying out two weeks at a time. Regardless, the city has never kept up with demand. Boys younger than Aidan have to try out for minor hockey because there's not enough ice time to go around, and the province just finished twinning Highway 63, the main highway in and out of the city.

Sixty-three has another nickname: "the Highway of Death." Wish I could say it's another stereotype, but this one earns its bad rap. I extricated eighteen dead, mangled bodies on that road last winter, and three dozen more survivors. If it's not passing a wide-load truck that gets them, it's a blizzard. If not a blizzard, ice. If not ice, then a shift-worker asleep at the wheel.

Highway 63 is Wood Buffalo's only access point, so I have to pass through the infamous route to reach every fire hall but 5, which is on the outskirts of town, just before the turnoff to 63, in a big open field, empty save for an identical-looking transit garage and, across Airport Road, upper-middle-class townhouses in the new neighbourhood of Prairie Creek. The morning of May 2, like many before, I steered the Tacoma into the lot, parked in the captain stall and carried my bag inside the wood-panelled building.

While our other halls have five bay doors, this one has fourteen, and inside the rest of its fifty thousand square feet is room for administration, mechanics and equipment for training the next generation of the Fort McMurray Fire Department. There's even a rock-climbing wall inside. It's also home to the Regional Emergency Operations Centre (REOC)—"the war room"—for whenever disaster might strike, with a seat for the mayor, fire chief, police chief and even liaisons from several oil companies. The city built hall 5 because they were expecting another thirty thousand people to move into the new subdivision between the hall and the airport. They budgeted for halls 6 and 7, too, but oil markets crashed, the industry hemorrhaged jobs, and real estate prices nosedived, putting the plans on hold. I've lived through three busts in my thirty-nine years. Such is life in the boom town.

I was born under the northern lights on April 24, 1977. When Mom was in labour, Dad was next door on construction of a larger hospital, dashing from work to the delivery room under the green streak in the sky above. There were so many babies on the way that mothers were wheeled into the corridors, and Mom's OB-GYN was also the town's emergency physician, running between howling women and whatever workplace injury awaited him. I hope the doctor enjoyed his retirement. Dad didn't. He had a massive heart attack at work in 2009 and died of heart complications a few years after his early retirement.

Like me, Dad was his own man and never needed to be part of a group setting to enjoy himself. Left alone in a mall, Dad would be lost in minutes, but you could drop him in the middle of the bush and he'd find his way out two days later, with a deer in tow. He loved his solitude, and even when he brought me along to hunt, we'd split up and not see each other again until it was time to light a campfire.

Personable isn't a word anyone used to describe my father—nor me, for that matter—but he was a keen helper, whether one needed a hand skinning game or running the barbecue at a school fundraiser. They simply needed to ask and he'd bend over backwards for them. But he was easygoing, which, admittedly, I am not always. I believe in rules, in the chain of command, in the right way and the wrong way of doing everything. My mom says that I see the world as black and white, and I have her to thank for that, though it took me a while to adopt her traits.

"Stay out of Snye Creek," she'd demand of little me. Imagine her surprise a week later when she found her twelve-year-old boy on the cover of *Fort McMurray Today*, splashing around in the Snye. Or there was the time in high school when a stranger in blue coveralls knocked on our door.

"Is Damian here?"

"Damian's in school," she said.

"Well, he won a draw to get his carpets steam-cleaned."

"What?" she yelled. "When? Where?" But she knew the answer: against her orders, I had skipped school to go to a trades expo, where I'd entered every draw. She scolded me for it later.

"Are you still getting your carpets cleaned?" I asked.

"You bet I am!"

That was the trouble I got into. Nothing too illicit. No DUIs or B&Es. Years of cadet training had instilled self-discipline and hard work in me, so my parents never had to worry about their boy selling dope behind Peter Pond Mall. Even if I did drink until four in the morning, Dad would be hovering over my bed two and a half hours later, shaking me awake and saying, "Come on, boy, it's time for chores." He had no issues with me enjoying myself, but he wanted me to know that come the morning, work always needed to be done, regardless of what had happened the night before. It made me who I am today: no matter how little sleep I've had, I'm up at six thirty the next day.

It also helped that from the time I was in size-two shoes, I needed to busy myself. As a kid I would wait by the window and watch to see if the neighbours had something for me to do. If someone was unloading rocks from their truck for landscaping, or stacking firewood for the winter, I was eager to help. My first job was sampling ice cream at a family friend's business; the perks were nice but the pay sucked and the work was too easy. I had a better time mowing my neighbour's lawn and shoveling his driveway. "I don't want to have to ask you to do it," he told me. "Just do it often and I'll pay you often."

My parents fully encouraged my restlessness by putting me to work inside the three-bedroom bungalow where they raised my younger sister, Danielle, and me. In the 1990s, ten years after the boom went bust, our parents didn't think they could hold on to their house any longer. By then, Dad's hours had been trimmed, which was good for his health, but Mom was raising us full-time and money was short. For Sale signs riddled front lawns all the way down to Franklin Avenue, the city's main street. A realtor took one look at the peeling linoleum floor and laminate cabinets in our home and shook her head. "See that house?" she said, pointing outside to an identical bungalow. "It's completely upgraded—and I still can't sell it, so how am I supposed to sell this?"

Dad put me in charge of upgrading the carpets, tiles and kitchen cabinetry. He trusted me because my only good grades were in shop class and I'd started collecting high school credits for work experience under Tim King of King Construction, a greying contractor who preferred to do everything himself than to call someone "boss." When my dad and I finished renovating, the agent was begging to represent us, but there was a problem: she valued the house at $80,000, the same price my parents had paid twelve years prior. So they hung on to it. Good thing, too—if Mom wanted to sell it today, it would go for a fair penny.

Architecture would've been my future if I'd had the attention span and patience for university—or the marks. I skidded by on low fifties through school, and my attendance rate was even worse. I liked climbing ladders with Tim more than sitting in desks. You'd figure the obvious plan B would be carpentry, but I'd talked to enough tradesmen to know there was more necessary desk-time to get my Red Seal than I was willing to commit to. Instead, I floated through my late teens and early twenties in Jasper National Park, where I discovered mountain climbing, one of a few sports I enjoy.

Most Canadian boys take to hockey, but in hockey the kid with the most money succeeds. He gets the extra ice time, the extra summer camp with professionals. The kid with the $400 stick has more chances to be better than the kid with the $100 stick. In mountain climbing, there's not much gear, so everyone is equal. And only you can push yourself to conquer something bigger, steeper, faster. The competition is between you and what's ahead. Of course, mountaineering wouldn't get me what I wanted—a good-paying job that didn't feel like a job, a big house and a happy family—but it grew my love for nature, and reminded me not to take the beauty of the boreal forest for granted when I returned home with some life direction.

I'd earned lifeguarding certificates through cadets, and following that, my emergency medical services training. Firefighting was a natural progression. In some fire halls, you meet guys who dressed as firemen when they were little and chased fire trucks on their trikes. For them, becoming a firefighter was destiny. For me, it was a rational decision. A decent salary for a hands-on job that scratched my helper itch.

At twenty, I phoned my mom to tell her my plans. "There's no way you'll pass the study," she said, mortified. The image of her only son running into an inferno wasn't what scared her. It was the textbooks.

She had a point. I've voluntarily read only two books in my life. Both were about Mount Everest, and each took me over a year to finish. Determined to make something of myself, I applied to fire school in Vermilion, near Edmonton . . . and was promptly rejected.

They accepted me the next year, after I took my emergency medical responder training. Burrowed in my dorm, my dirty blond mop of hair fell over my face as I pored over the texts, shutting myself out of the keggers down the hall in residence. The only things distracting me were the rosy cheeks of a bright-eyed girl in the residence halls.

Melanie was a marketing assistant at the Alberta Fire Training School, a small school where everyone knew everyone. She was outgoing and good-hearted, and I admired the hell out of her independence. Sometimes she'd leave the raging party next door just to say hi and offer me a study break. There was never a sweeter girl.

We dated for a few months, but split after I returned to Fort McMurray to start my career—or at least try. The fire department wasn't hiring. Nobody was, because in 1999 the economy was still in the toilet. I worked construction before getting hired as a private firefighter on a gas refinery in Southern Alberta. It was dreadful. They hardly let me piss without taking a safety course and passing through two checkpoints.

I eventually landed a coveted job with the municipality in 2001. When I returned to Vermilion to upgrade my training two years later, Melanie was on her way to Australia to live for an indefinite period as a beach bum. We stayed in touch, but I wouldn't see her again until 2005. By then the Iraq War had destabilized the oil market, causing the price of a barrel of oil to soar. The strenuous and expensive task of turning bitumen tar into petroleum made financial sense again, and Fort McMurray's population surged like never before, attracting labourers and service workers from all over the world. By the time Melanie and I rekindled the flame, my FMFD helmet's leather badge, with my member number 209, had four years of soot stains. At the end of every tour—two day shifts followed by two night shifts—I'd hang my helmet in my red locker and drive straight to Melanie for my four days off.

We were older now, in our late twenties, and all that time as friends had primed us for each other's personality. So she knew what she was getting into in January 2006, just three months into our rekindled relationship, when I proposed and she said yes. By May, she'd quit her job and moved to be with me in Fort McMurray. We married in Costa Rica that October, and on our honeymoon we were pregnant. Friends must have thought we were nuts, but building a future with Melanie was no different than anything else: You look at what's in front of you and get it done.

Two dozen framed photos of graduating classes furnish the entry to the captains' office in Hall 5. Each class is larger than the one before it, from six recruits in 2001 to nine in 2010 to fourteen in 2016. I glanced at the latest batch of probationary firefighters and didn't recognize a single fresh-faced "probie," whose member badges were now in the 590s. Not that the graduates in between 209 and 590 all stayed in town—FMFD is treated as the farm team of fire departments, a training ground for the rest of Canada. Guys come and go for many reasons: they can't get used to the northern lifestyle, the isolation gets to them, or there just aren't enough gals in town to settle down with (the male-to-female population is rumoured to be three to one). The high turnaround is a struggle from time to time, but new faces bring new opportunities. As a captain, I know that wherever the probies end up, people's lives will be in their hands, so I'm determined they leave us as the most disciplined workers our profession offers.

Captain Ryan Pitchers was stacking paperwork when I entered our office. Pitchers is one of my oldest friends, going back to our time together in air cadets. But while I simply internalized the regiment training and transferred it to lifeguarding, he followed through and enlisted in the army. He's a bulky, bald man who joined the department in 2000 after a tour in Bosnia. Like me, he takes the stripes on his navy blue uniform as seriously as an army sergeant. He has a soft spot, though—Pitchers is a sucker for animals and runs a pet shop on the side. A lot of the older guys in the department have side jobs, including me; not only do I protect houses, I still build them through my side business, D's Custom Woodworks.

"Morning," I said, setting my duffel bag on a chair. "How was B-Shift?"

"Long night," he said, concentrating on the files. "Wildfire got too close for comfort. Pumper 4 soaked it good, but they needed extra men for the cleanup. Our boys didn't get back till the morning."

"This the fire out west?"

"One of 'em," he said, glancing up. "That's by Horse River, Alberta Forestry's bag—they're on top of it now. But we've been doing lots of overtime laying waterlines in Prairie Creek; left a decent creek along the highway—they might have to name it after someone. The equine club needed some help getting their animals out. Should've seen Firefighter Stephenson manhandling this mustang into a trailer."

"Bet he could've knocked it out cold."

"If he wanted to."

"Did you get civilians out?"

"Negative," said Ryan. "Mayor gave evacuation orders for Prairie Creek and Gregoire, but by the time we got back here, three or four maybe, she lifted the orders. Temperatures dropped, chilled it out. Still burning, as you can see, but water-bombers will finish the job."

Normally I'd have been on top of all this, but I took the Sunday off to drive the family to St. Albert for a dance competition. Aidan is in competitive dance, and is proving himself to be quite the performer. His team won a small treasure chest of medals, and by the time we got back to Saprae Creek, it was midnight.

"You said there's another wildfire?" I asked.

"Up north, TaigaNova woods, probably ATVs," he said. All-terrain vehicles—quads, trikes—are one of the main causes of brush fires. In this town, with all the disposable income, the vehicles are as abundant as running water. And after such a dry winter, hardly anybody could wait to whip 'em out. It just takes one spark from a backfiring muffler to scorch the earth.

Pitchers continued, "That one was a close call—burned to city limits. They diverted bombers from Horse River right to the edge of town there. Woykin"—as in our battalion chief Mike Woykin—"said they had two crews trying to convince these shops in a strip mall to close while embers hailed down on them. The owners thought they could put out the hot spots themselves with buckets of water. Anyway, it's out now, but there's a hell of a lot of ash and debris to shovel."

I thanked Pitchers for the update and entered the captains' dorm at the back of the office, took off my hoodie and khakis and had a hot shower. I unzipped my bag and pulled out two clean uniforms, folded so you could see the Canadian flag on the chest. I always bring a second one. As a member of an integrated department, I'm a firefighter as well as an EMT, and it's impossible to predict what I might be wiping off my clothes at the end of a shift—projectile vomit from teenage girls, crap from the sick or elderly who couldn't get out of bed, the putrid smell of a house fire. I've lost count of how many suicides I've cleaned up after—and those calls never get any easier—but I've got nine notches on my belt for every baby I've delivered in the field.

I buttoned my shirt and pants, fastened my FMFD belt buckle, grabbed a sack of oatmeal from my bag and strode to the kitchen. A debate in the lounge detoured me. No surprise, it was Chris Relph, an eight-year firefighter pacing the floor, and Kyle Hitchcock, a seven-year firefighter, who was taking the green team's beating with more grace. (That's about the extent of my NHL knowledge: there's the Edmonton Oilers, the Calgary Flames and then a bunch of other-coloured jerseys I don't recognize.) I stuck my six-foot-one frame in front of the flat screen, pretending I was oblivious to the fact that these guys are the biggest sports fanatics in our department and never miss a practice with the department hockey team, the Pylons. "Oh, hey guys, what's going on?" I teased.

"Cap, come on!" pleaded Relph, furrowing his thick dark brows.

"What? Is there something happening behind me?" I turned three-sixty, nodding as I faced them again. "Oh, organized men's fig-ure skating. My favourite." They rolled their eyes, having seen my bit a hundred times before.

"Sorry, Cap," Relph apologized. "It was a long and busy night, so we missed the game."

"So I've heard. They gonna need extra men for cleanup?" I asked.

"Maybe a couple firefighters," Hitchcock advised.

I nodded. "Good to see you back," I told him.

Hitchcock had just come back after tearing his acromioclavicular joint at the top of his shoulder during a Pylons game. "Great to be back," Hitchcock replied.

You can quickly sort the get-it-done from the get-it-done-better boys, the type who return from a call and say, "Wow, that's new—better study up," and hit the books (instead of wishing for better luck next time). They've also got the right heart for the team. Hitchcock is damn passionate and is the first to step up to a task, even if it's washing the rims. Relph is a prankster, famous for sending embarrassing department-wide emails from your account if you didn't log out—asking the captain for advice on hemorrhoid medication, for instance. But after you're done blushing, he'll ask how your wife and kids are, and he always remembers your birthday. That little stuff goes a long way.

Relph and Hitchcock arrived as new recruits when I was an officer-in-training—the same place Relph is now as an acting captain—so I don't mind getting friendly. Still, as an officer, you're taught to distance yourself from non-officers, to crack the whip if they're goofing around or sit them on the bumper and soak them in shame if they're too slow with the hose. I'd never had to put these boys on the bumper, but I'd definitely barked at them a few times.

Once, when Hitchcock was still a new firefighter, I hired him on one of my house jobs. "You ever lay hardwood before?" I asked after a shift.

"Not once in my life," he said.

"Wanna make some extra cash?"

For three days I showed him how to measure, cut and lay a Brazilian walnut flown in for our deputy chief's abode. Hitchcock was intimidated but patient, and after covering three thousand square feet we'd bonded over our families and I'd learned about his high school sweetheart who followed him from Ontario. The next day, at the hall, he was showing around a probie and introduced me as "Damian."

My eyes turned to stone. "It's Lieutenant Asher."

Hitchcock, pale as snow, said, "Yes, sir," and shuffled away.

Later I explained to him that, around the hall, and especially in front of probies, he needed to call me by my title so the new crew members would know the authority hierarchy. They needed to see the stripes. Now it's Relph and Hitchcock's turn to get respect from their upper peers and subordinates, to set the example for those who will follow them. My job, as an officer, is to lead calls, educate and make sure everyone's safe. Truck checks are especially essential— can't let my guys get to a scene unprepared. But sweeping out a corner of the hall or cleaning the cupboards? Making sure the floor's mopped and truck's scrubbed daily? It's on them, as seniors, to make sure the basics get done.

Relph and Hitchcock were having a harder time than me, though. The department had grown so fast that crews blew up in size and juniors started outnumbering seniors. Guys got early promotions. How do you reprimand and corral five probies when you're not much older or more experienced than them yourself? If you leave it to the one officer, everyone assumes he's a tyrant and the officer struggles for respect.

With fifteen minutes in their shift to spare, Relph and Hitchcock checked the sinks, floors and dorms to make sure everything was spotless.

Inside the kitchen, cabinets and fridge doors slammed and creaked as B-Shift, the night crew, cleared the room for A-shift, my guys. Every shift starts with a forty-minute table talk over breakfast, while the captain gives the lineup and order of the day. I waited at the head of a boardroom table while my oatmeal soaked and my crew settled in with their smoothies and power drinks. There were nine of them, all cut like steel. This new generation loves to work out. It's made the annual firemen's calendar a profitable fundraiser.

"Jamieson," I said, pointing my pen to Joe Jamieson. "You're on Pumper 5 with Morari, Hovagimian and Cseke." Jamieson is a

Toronto boy who traded out his preppy-boy look for some neck stubble and shaggy hair once he got a lay of the hinterland. Even with his quasi-backwoods look, few ladies would say no to him. Good looks and confidence aside, he joined us through a program for people with life experience and was hired without training. As a former plumber, he knew his way around tools and structures. Better yet, he had the right attitude. He isn't too proud to say, "I don't know—teach me."

Tia Morari was quite the opposite—when she started, she thought she knew everything and had to show it. Today she's one of our fiercest seniors, but when she walked onto the floor seven years ago, she was a Saskatchewan girl with a trucker's mouth fresh out of school and ready to conquer the industry—not the first job in her life, but the first of this nature. Once, as a probie in her first year, Morari did an in-service presentation to a group of seniors on vertical ventilation. She stood in front of the PowerPoint, botching the basics. "Stop," I interrupted. "Just stop right now." I pulled her aside and laid out my expectations in no uncertain terms. I'm known to ride the juniors and set high expectations, but I might have been too rough that time. I'd never have to do that again, though. In spite of her shaky start, she stuck her head in the books and emerged as one of the top firefighters in the department. Not only that, but Morari took a few cues from me; she's first to tell a probie to shut his mouth, first to shake her head and ask, "What the hell were you thinking?" She'll make a great captain when her time comes in a couple years.

"Morari," I called out. "You're operating."

I lined up the rest of the firefighter, paramedic and EMT roles, and then laid out the day. "Who needs to go to the gym?" Four hands rose. "You guys cool with a one thirty workout?"

"Yessir," said Trevor Shantz, a freckled and short youngster. He'd been hired four years ago, at nineteen, and was a strong worker, partly thanks to the mentorship from his brother-in-law, Chris Relph. Still, you've got to knock these kids down sometimes.

"Not you, Shantz," I said. "Pump 4's still in TaigaNova. I'm sending you and Robinson for cleanup after training." Shantz and another grunt nodded dutifully. "So, we'll check the trucks, train until lunch, work out and then the afternoon's yours. Okay?"

I waited for confirmation but the kitchen was silent, everyone's gaze fixed behind me outside the window. There were four plumes now, joined at the heads in a stack effect where smoke hit the air current. The sky had an orange overcast, and their faces looked grim. "The Beast," as history would come to know it, was growing.

CHAPTER 2

ACTIVATING THE WAR ROOM

Before it was the Beast, the fire was MWF-009, the ninth Mc-Murray wildfire of the season, logged by Alberta Agriculture and Forestry at 16:08 on Sunday, May 1. Also known as the Horse River Fire, it was the size of four football fields when discovered. Sounds massive, but a year prior, flames had torched five times more timber south of Saprae Creek, prompting the Regional Municipality of Wood Buffalo to call for a voluntary evacuation of our hamlet. Our family had respected the order and packed our bags, pets and an emergency binder of important paperwork—insurance policies, passports and such. In a day, a cavalry of heavy machinery, three choppers, a tanker and twenty firefighters beat the fire, which had reached eight hundred metres from the edge of our hamlet. The kids were playing in the basement by noon the next day.

On Sunday night, as MWF-009 swelled to one hundred hectares, the city ordered about five thousand folks to leave some southwest neighbourhoods and campsites, and they prepared MacDonald Island Park Recreation Centre for emergency refuge. Mayor Melissa Blake declared a local state of emergency, automatically making Darby Allen, our fire chief, the city's new boss—chief of emergency management whenever the natural order is suspended. Mac Island had sheltered people recently: in 2013, when the Hangingstone

River flooded. So the Horse River wildfire gave us no reason to panic. Still, it continued to grow, to one hundred and fifty hectares in one night, and required four choppers, two tankers and other apparatus from smaller Northern Alberta communities nearby. Dozers worked around the clock on swaths of lumber to keep the flames at bay, as did firefighters soaking up the west side of Highway 63. They must have made headway because at 3 a.m. officials downgraded evacuation orders in the southwest neighbourhood of Gregoire to a "shelter in place." Basically, have your bags packed but keep calm and carry on. The orders for Prairie Creek, where hall 5 resides, were stayed, but only for civilian homes, of which there weren't many in the young and underdeveloped neighbourhood. By Monday morning, astute McMurrayites, those who recognized the towering white clouds, filled up their tanks and gathered their belongings.

The recipe for wildfires is as simple as mac 'n' cheese, with just three ingredients: ignition, fuel and weather.

Ignition is simple. A lightning strike or a careless campfire can spark a blaze that scorches a few hectares in a matter of hours. MWF-009 was possibly caused by an off-road vehicle that spit flaming dry, organic material caught under the engine into the grass.

When it comes to fuel, there's no shortage, and the biggest supply, black spruce, is particularly volatile. A fire-adapted species that spreads its seeds through blazes, its chemical makeup primes it for burning. Aspens and poplars are more resistant, but altogether, boreal forests need fire like rainforests need rain. It's essential to the propagation and renewal process.

The last part of the recipe, weather, has another triangle of ingredients within it: heat, relative humidity and wind.

We're acclimatized to seven-month winters up here, but thanks to the warm El Niño drafts, every snowfall of late 2015 and early 2016 disappeared within weeks. The snowmelt drained into our rivers and creeks instead of the frosted earth, which would otherwise have absorbed precipitation, moistened and guarded us from wildfires. Then came the hottest and driest spring on record. Even the bogs were dry as tinder. May 2 had reached twenty-seven degrees Celsius, a temperature high rarely recorded in summer, let alone spring, and by that Monday, there'd already been 370 provincial wildfires, more than double as many as the same time in 2015.

> The recipe for wildfires is as simple as mac 'n' cheese, with just three ingredients: ignition, fuel and weather.

When the Horse River Fire flared up, high winds spread flames from tree to tree and embers from grassland to grassland at a wicked pace. But they blew southwest, away from town, so as long as the winds didn't change direction the chain of command felt it was reckless to sound the alarms. Sure enough, Environment Canada's own data said the wind direction would stay put and even relax. I wanted my men to prepare regardless, though, so, on the morning of May 2, after truck check, it was time for forestry practice.

We hauled a red utility trailer into the adjacent bush on Airport Road and familiarized the crew with the gear. Set up the pumps and drafting mechanisms. Laid out all hoses and splitters. Found a water source and filled the pumpkins—orange rubber bladders you can pump with hundreds of gallons of water from a creek, then deflate and fold up like a sleeping bag when you're finished. I walked them through maintenance and tested their troubleshooting skills.

"Get Mark-3," I said to Shantz, referring to a forestry pump. He climbed into the thirty-foot trailer to lift it from a top cabinet.

"Sure you can reach that?" asked Morari. Shantz might be the only guy in the unit she's got an inch on, but he took it in good fun and returned with the lightweight pump. They huddled as I taught how to disassemble it in the field. "If it sucks up gravel, it's screwed. But you can take this right in half." I twisted the built-in wrench to crack open the red casing. "Dig it out, change the gasket and snap it back together. That's all stuff in the manual."

I may have read only two books in thirty-nine years, but in the last fifteen, I've read the manual on every apparatus cover-to-cover. Frankly, I don't understand why you wouldn't. In the distance, smoke was thickening now. It was early afternoon, and as the temperature rose, the fire grew. "Guys," I barked. "Focus."

We were prepping chicken pesto pizza for lunch when dispatch called. A house fire alarm in Gregoire, one of the southwest neighbourhoods with a shelter-in-place order. We turned the stovetops off and stormed into the bay, past the ambulance, ladder trucks, tankers and light rescues. At the first vehicle in line—Pumper 5, a top-of-the-line truck with a large cab for five men—I jumped into my bunker boots and pants by the side door, pulled up the suspenders, threw on a tan bunker jacket and jumped in the passenger seat with my helmet in my lap. Morari grabbed the wheel and raced out.

The block in Gregoire was hazier than the rest of town, but the brush fire was way out of view. Still, a piece of burning ember can fly miles. All it takes is one ember the size of a gumdrop landing on a roof to bring a house to rubble—and spread to the next. The majority of alarm calls we go to are false. Regardless, we always prepare for the worst, clothed in bunker gear with a breathing apparatus strapped to our backs, even though, as we parked in front of the house trailer, we saw no smoke or flames to speak of. While Jamieson rang the bell and banged on the door, I circled the structure.

As a captain, my primary decision after a three-sixty walk-around is whether I'm going to send guys in or not. That's on me. Someone goes in and doesn't come out—on me. A firefighter's kids grow up never knowing their father or mother—on me. I read up on case studies often, but nothing has prepared me better than contracting. When I show up on site, I can almost draw a floor plan of the structure just from what I see on the outside. I know the solid points of a house, where the load beams are, where the weak points are. I know where firefighters should stand, where they shouldn't. I know how loads are affected by heat and how the house will move under the attack of a fire. I never have to go into it blind.

Whatever caused the alarm, it wasn't showing from the outside. But peering into the windows, I could see one of the rooms was steaming, making it difficult to know whether a civilian was inside it. In which case, we'd have to go in.

After a minute of banging on the door and no answer, Jamieson asked me, "Should we break it down?"

"Try before you pry," I said, reciting an industry mantra. He turned the doorknob—it was unlocked—and shrugged.

The screeching smoke detectors were inaudible over the pounding bass from a stereo in a room, where steam billowed out its ajar door. Jamieson nudged it wide and called again: "Fire department— sorry!"

You couldn't hear the tunes or the detectors anymore. Just a woman shrieking.

The men and I turned our backs with a smatter of "sorries" and "sorry, ma'ams," while Morari handed her a bath towel. Once the tattooed lady had wrapped herself and her embarrassment had passed, I escorted her to her smoke detector for an important lesson.

"Ma'am," I said, patiently as possible, "there are two types of detectors: photoelectric and ionizing. What you've got here is a photoelectric device. It sends out a beam of light, times how long it takes for that light to beam back, and if it gets caught in anything at all—like maybe shower steam—it calls us. The other one detects dust and smoke. I'm not telling you to take cold showers, but an ionizing detector costs fourteen dollars. Buy one."

> It's not always something shocking that touches your soul. Just something relatable.

Most house calls are false alarms, but truthfully, when we're racing to a scene we're half praying for that. The number of first responders with PTSD is scary. Some unions have called it a crisis, and the efforts to build peer groups and counselling stations for these stressed individuals can't come fast enough. We cope with a healthy dose of black humour, but sometimes after a gory sight, I'll call in a firefighter and say, "If you need someone to talk to, the help is there. Don't bottle it up."

It's not always something shocking that touches your soul. Just something relatable. For me, it was a standard suicide call in 2014. An eighty-five-year-old man entered his garage in the middle of the night and hanged himself. His little old lady of a wife found him and called 9-1-1.

My dad had died a month prior, so after confirming that the man wasn't breathing and breaking the news to his wife, it felt like I was telling Mom that Dad was dead all over again. The old lady leaned on me and squeezed my hands. "Please, please," she said and quivered, "check one more time. I don't know what I'll do without him."

It was my thirteenth year in the field. Until then, nothing had shaken me.

Most of the gang hit the gym after eating, but I hung back in the kitchen to reread the pumpkins manual with the radio on. All the exercise and heavy lifting I need to stay fit I get from home-building. Between the construction business and firefighting, plus Melanie's home fitness classes, I was optimistic about my dream of "Freedom Forty." Not a full freedom—I'm way too restless for that. But I hoped it would be my last build for a while. Soon I could focus just on the department and make good on my promise to Melanie that we'd travel the world one day.

The country station broke from the tunes to give their concerned listeners an update on the fire. The TaigaNova Fire was held, they said, but the Horse River Fire was 1.5 kilometres from Highway 63 and Airport Road—from us at hall 5. Outside the kitchen windows, a caravan of high-end trucks and SUVs parked in the lot, and one by one, McMurray's top brass entered the building.

There was Melissa Blake, our mayor of twelve years, marching to the main entry. She's a homespun hockey mom—a favourite of the family-focused McMurrayites—who's pissed off a lot of lefties with what they see as indifference to climate change. But what do you expect? We have the oil sands to thank for the highest salaries in the nation, so don't act shocked that she's industry-friendly.

Fire Chief Darby Allen followed the mayor. Chief Allen came to us from Hampshire, England, by way of Calgary. He'd never lived in a small city before, but the people embraced the soft-spoken English-man with over three decades of service. At fifty-nine, I guessed his retirement wasn't far off.

By the time I noticed Alberta forestry manager Bernie Schmitte, manager of the water treatment plant Guy Jette, and Michael Powlesland, the procurement supervisor, I had a good idea of what was going on. The war room had been activated.

The REOC is a one-thousand-square-foot windowless room with wall-to-wall whiteboards, charts and maps. It used to be at the provincial building downtown, and the only time this updated space had been used was during simulation training in February. Naturally, it was for a mock wildfire disaster, a scenario in which flames were breaching city limits but not actually catching houses. The senior managers of Wood Buffalo's major branches were mostly taught about organizational structure—who reports to whom. The REOC is very regimented, because everybody has a role to play. The challenging part is sticking to that role, which might not be your expertise but rather whatever's required of you. The simulation threw curveballs at the managers to see if they would honour the hierarchy.

When I took the elevator to the second floor for a view inside, twenty-some office chairs had coloured vests waiting on their backrests: blue for Planning, red for Logistics, orange for Operations, green for Command. Allen pulled one of two green vests over his uniform and circled the Wood Buffalo map where MWF-009 burned. Half a dozen other people I didn't know either scribbled data on a whiteboard or talked into desk phones. Powlesland, made chief of logistics in these circumstances, negotiated deals with heavy equipment and water vendors to relieve the city of any red tape during a worst-case scenario. It was all very mundane for a so-called "state of emergency."

> The REOC is very regimented, because everybody has a role to play.

"Asher," somebody called behind me. It was Jody Butz, the assistant deputy chief of operations, en route to REOC. "How's it going?"

His question surprised me. "I was going to ask you the same thing."

"We activated yesterday evening, you didn't hear?" he asked. I told him about the dance competition. "Same here, was coming home from Edmonton with the new RV when I got the call. Things were looking pretty dicey—I'm running the firefighting department until the state of emergency is called off, but I don't think it'll be too much longer."

"Why's that?"

"Well," he said, trying not to sound too sure of himself, "I got up in the chopper this morning, didn't look so bad. Fire's got about a click, two clicks from city limits, but it's manageable."

"Where's Forestry with it?" I asked.

"Spread to eighteen hundred acres but they can contain it. Dozers are working around the fire's edge, making a break. They've got a good head start."

"Do they? The boys are getting a bit worked up over it."

"Tell me about it," he said. "Social media is losing its mind right now. But it's still west of the Athabasca. Long as that river stays put, I think we're fine."

Butz had a point. The Athabasca is a kilometre wide, and in all my years, of all the fires I'd seen, flames had never jumped it. A few spot fires, sure, but those were manageable so long as you had ground crew at the ready with piss-packs, rubber backpacks that shoot water out of a reflex-action nozzle and make us look like Ghostbusters.

"We'll be ready," I said, shaking Butz's hand and wishing him luck before returning to the elevator. When the hatches opened, a girl charged out and crashed into me. "Sorry," she cried.

"You all right?" She was frazzled, lost and way overdressed for this town, wearing a neat blouse and colourful blazer.

"My name's Michaela. I'm the emergency management summer intern from Victoria. Today's my first day."

"Well, it looks like you're getting thrown right into it. Just keep calm and follow directions, and I'm sure you'll be fine. There are a lot of experienced people up there."

During the last few hours of Monday, text messages buzzed and pinged so much that Hall 5 sounded like a video game. Normally, when I catch guys who seem underworked, I call them into my office, slide a blank paper and pen across my desk and tell them to write down every piece of equipment on the truck—down to every pencil in the glovebox. Or, I'll bring them into the bay, take apart a chainsaw and say, "Put it together. . . . Now do it with gloves on. . . . Now do it with your eyes closed. Why? Because it gets dark outside, that's why."

This was different, though. Nobody was disinterested in fire-fighting. It was the opposite; the crew was hopped up on adrenaline, reading social media posts about burning houses and other crap. I kept reminding them: We're the Fort McMurray Fire Department. When there's a fire in Fort McMurray, we're the first to know.

Crew had crowded by a window, watching the top brass standing atop the brick hose tower. The tower is for dangling wet hoses after a battle for drying, but at thirty-five feet tall, it's one of the best vantage points outside downtown Fort McMurray. "Come on," I said. I led Joe, Tia, Cseke and the rest of them up the tower for a view of the fire. It was almost the end of shift, and I wanted to make sure they'd take the message to their families that there was nothing to panic over.

It felt as if someone was holding a blow dryer to the back of my head as I stepped on deck. The temperature was double what it was the same time last year. Beyond the industrial park, over the hills, columns of smoke had grown tall and fluffy and blotted together like dirty cotton balls. The glow of flames painted the edges of the charcoal clouds and western horizon a milky orange.

> The glow of flames painted the edges of the charcoal clouds and western horizon a milky orange.

"Looks fierce, doesn't it?" I admitted. "But, look—" I raised an index finger to the southern rim of the smoke and held it there for thirty seconds, letting the dark mass pass behind it. "See where it's headed? South. That's good." I traced the hill with the same finger. "You've got a huge power line there. That's a great firebreak. In front of it, you've got Hangingstone and the Horse. Two river valleys. Even better firebreaks. Then you've got the Athabasca. Any of you ever tip a canoe in that and had the pleasure of swimming to shore?" I paused. "Yeah, no fun. So I know this looks big and scary, but they've got everything on it. Tonight, the temperature will cool and squeeze it down. Forestry will go for the kill in the morning."

The crew got it now. After everyone descended the tower, I lifted my phone to the sky, waited for the flea-sized water-bombers to fly into my viewfinder and snapped a photo that I texted to Melanie.

Nice view

Should I be concerned?

No be home in an hour

When I got home, Melanie told me the Saprae Creek community page on Facebook was overflowing with fearful rumours. I'm almost never on social media, but it seemed like a good time to log on to balm the frenzy.

I sat at a computer in the TV room and typed:

I'm a fire captain with the city. If you haven't seen it already, the municipality has a Twitter page of all up-to-date info on the fires. It will be factual info, not what has been passed around and exploded on social media. Always being prepared is never a bad thing. The fire department and forestry are on scene doing everything possible to keep the residents of all the communities safe.

CHAPTER 3

A FALSE SENSE OF SECURITY

The brisk night air had subdued the Beast, or so it appeared from my bedroom window when I woke up on Tuesday, May 3, to a clear blue dawn. I deactivated the alarm clock on my phone before it sounded, and set it on the nightstand where I keep my wedding ring. A dull platinum band with curved lines I designed myself, my ring doesn't just represent my marriage but also family. It was the middle of a tour, though, with two more night shifts before my days off. As a safety measure to prevent pinching during vehicle extrications, the wedding band spends more time in the top drawer than it does on my left hand.

A lot of guys dread night shifts. It should come as no shock the field attracts thrill-seekers, who are sorely disappointed when they realize 80 percent of night shifts are spent waiting around for a call. And when you're young, you want to party every evening, so not only are they bored, they're filled with FOMO—fear of missing out. I was one of them, but now I prefer overnighters because they give me the early mornings with my kids, and then I can get to building houses while the sun's up.

At 6:30 a.m. I was ready to roll, even if the family wasn't. Soon, Melanie's alarm clock would ring. I let her rest, kissing her before entering the en suite bathroom. Warm water filled my permanently curved hands (twenty straight years of hammering and sawing will curl your fingers into half a bowl), and I washed my face on my side of the vanity. After my morning shave, scraping each follicle to the top of my ears, I woke the kids for school.

Aidan is like me and awakens with a full tank of fuel. Soon as his eyes open, there's no going back, and two taps on his door is all it took for him to start rummaging for an outfit, wash, brush his teeth and dress himself without another order. "Thanks, Dad," he said. I gave him a thumbs-up as I walked to his sister's room down the hall.

Taya, on the other hand, moves at a snail's pace, even after eleven hours of sleep. After I shook her awake, she slumped out of the bed I built—a solid oak and maple crib conversion, no different than her brother's—and plopped firmly on the ground, where she peeled off her pyjamas as if they were Super Glued. "Get up. Get dressed. Get going," I commanded, each time with a soft kick to her butt while she grumbled and whined. I threw a mismatched tank top and shorts at her. "Ten minutes, then breakfast. Got it, miss?" She nodded grumpily.

Through the double doors that divide the house in two wings—sleeping quarters and living quarters—I descended the short steps into the sunken great room and ascended into our massive kitchen. The island stretches twenty-four feet across and is our preferred spot for meals, although there's a breakfast nook and dining room on either side of it. But I didn't design the house for us. Not entirely.

I'll always imagine the prospective buyer before I draw up plans. The first house I built for myself, a small bungalow in Timberlea, a boom-time subdivision in the early 2000s, was designed with a young couple in mind: eleven hundred square feet with a decent kitchen, a master bedroom, a guest room and the rest of it left open. I sold it to newlyweds for $400,000 and moved on to the next build: a two-storey with a bonus room above the garage. This one I envisioned as an entertaining house for a mature couple. The kitchen had a twenty-four-foot bar for amazing parties. One Christmas, Melanie and I had forty people over with plenty of room to spare. After Taya was born, we sold it for $850,000 to my mom's hairdresser. An incremental gain. But the next buyer in mind was a huge leap forwards. I pictured the CEO of an oil service company with grown-up children attending Keyano College.

When I showed Melanie the forty-two-hundred-square-foot plans she almost smacked me. "That is way too extravagant," she spat. "And how long will it take?"

Three years. Most of it done myself—just as Tim King of King Construction had taught me. It was somewhat of a sideshow for friends and colleagues, who'd come by unannounced to marvel at its size, or, when it was finished, to bring their visiting relatives as if it were a tourist attraction.

The travertine tiles were imported from Turkey. The kids each have a walk-in closet and a full bathroom, and our own bathroom has a rain shower that you could practically play street hockey in. The basement is one part rec room, with a poker and pool table (though I'm not a pool shark and would probably lose the kids' college funds before I knew a winning poker hand), one part crafts room for the wife and kids, and one part home business— there's an exercise studio for Melanie's personal training and fusion fitness classes. I did all the fancy upgrades (coffered ceilings, custom columns in open rooms) inside, and outside, on two acres surrounded by thirty-foot-tall young poplars, I built a four-bay garage with a second-floor apartment, knowing anyone of wealth will need to store a lot of toys: boats, campers, Ski-Doos, ATVs.

People often ask me why I did it all myself. There's a joy in construction that only people who enjoy dirty work can understand—that at the end of every day, you see actual progress. Some people have data-entry jobs where they do the same thing day in, day out and never witness the big picture of what they're picking at, but in one day I can complete a whole aspect of a house. There's a therapeutic side to the physical labour too—even something as simple as moving a pile of dirt from one place to another is satisfying. Sure, a Bobcat would be great in that scenario, but if all I had was a five-gallon pail, I'd still get the job done. I feel the same way at the fire hall scrubbing trucks or mopping floors. But the act of creating is especially fulfilling, and after three years on the Saprae Creek acreage, I'd created something amazing.

The last property assessment from the city had pegged the place at $1.8 million—all we'd need for Freedom Forty. That is, if I could ever convince Melanie to let us sell. Once the house was inhabitable, she'd done a complete one-eighty. We had occupied the finished house on Christmas Eve 2014, and for the better half of the thirty-six months leading up to that point, I had been in the same orange hoodie and muddy khakis. I'd change into them after a night shift and get right back to work at 8 a.m., even if a hellish accident on Highway 63 had kept me up all night. I could go four days straight without seeing the family. For a decade, Melanie had been asking when we would get downtime. I could finally say we were almost there. *Almost.* There was still work to be done on the yard, which I'd start that morning.

Aidan was half done with his cereal by the time Taya sauntered in and pulled up a stool. "Are you ready for school?" I asked.

"Yep." The word popped from her mouth like a bubble.

"Did you brush your teeth?"

"Nope."

"Did you wash your hands?"

"Nooo."

"Did you wash your face?"

She blinked her green eyes as if I'd spoken Swahili. It'd be hard to remember she's my daughter, but she is a spitting image of Melanie.

"Well," I said, shaking my head, "I thought you were ready."

"Well," she said back, mockingly, "nobody told me to do those things."

"Taya," Aidan interrupted, pushing up his glasses like an unimpressed accountant. "It's the same thing every morning, nobody has to tell you to do those things. You just do them." My proud boy. He acts like me, and his round, ruddy face and light blond hair resemble mine too.

Melanie got up just in time to walk the kids to the school bus at the end of the road with me. We saw half our neighbours there, dropping seven kids off between them all, and because I was their go-to fireman, they asked me for my opinion on the wildfire. I paused for a sense of the wind. It wasn't extreme, but it wasn't pushing southwest anymore, either. It had changed directions, pushing north, which wasn't altogether terrible news so long as it didn't shift eastwards. The sky was blue, but choppers flew back and forth with giant buckets of water, meaning there had to be something below the trees worth fighting. "Best to keep your grasses and any high-hazard areas watered—up to fifteen feet in your trees. Any fuel you've got in your yards, any barrels or jerry-cans, keep it in your garage."

They seemed unconvinced. "Good news is the smoke is coming from the west flank of the river and we are way east," I continued. "I haven't been out there, but I know fire crews are on the ground and cleaning up any hot spots east of the river. For any more updates, check the municipal website. Okay?" The parents thanked me, the bus left, and we headed back to our not-so-humble abode.

Between the summer bonfire parties, movie nights, Easter egg hunts and holiday events at the community hall, I've made bonds with nearly all nine hundred residents of Saprae Creek Estates. From the end of the road, I can point and name every owner of every house in two wide cul-de-sacs. Our nearest neighbour's teenage daughters baby-sit our kids, and another neighbour, Pam, is their school librarian. With two jobs and two kids, I have little time for friends, but Melanie and I have built a good sense of community here.

> From the end of the road, I can point and name every owner of every house in two wide cul-de-sacs.

Now that Taya had started Grade 1, Melanie was thinking of returning to full-time work. She had an interview scheduled that morning for a job as the RCMP's police clerk, plus yoga and a big grocery run to take advantage of it being Discount Tuesday. I'd have all morning and most of the afternoon to myself, to water and mow the mustard-coloured lawn, organize the mess of tools from construction and lay topsoil over the patches that suffered most from a winter that never was and a spring that had hardly sprung. Soon I'd get the fence up, and my grand opus would be done.

I fed our two rag-doll kittens, let out our ten-year-old chocolate lab Petzl, filled a thermos with creamy coffee and carried a stereo to the yard for news updates in between Keith Urban and Carrie Underwood songs. The 93.3 Country DJs were optimistic in light of the panic flooding locals' social media. Along with Gregoire's residents, Prairie Creek's could return to their homes now, they said. The RV park was still under mandatory evacuation, but the DJs highlighted the good progress our firefighters had made protecting the highway, and the fireguards that were now in place. The wind forecast was uncertain, either south-southeast, away from the city, or south-southwest, towards a small population of the city. So long as people had their belongings in order, they should be able to make a careful and immediate exit if the situation got sketchier.

For two hours, I cleaned up the acreage; tucked the construction equipment, wheelbarrows, ladders and kids' toys against the shop; and rotoraked the dead grass. All around me, neighbours did the same, prepping their yards for May long weekend barbecues. But their body language showed unease as the sky turned a blueish orange and the sense of comfort they'd had that morning wavered. At 11 a.m., the music abruptly stopped to announce Mayor Melissa Blake's live media briefing. I turned off the lawn mower and dialled up the volume.

"Here we are on another day that's filled with heat, sunshine and a little smoke in the air," she said. Blake is famous for her cheeriness, so I took her tone with a healthy dose of skepticism. She said the fire had choked off the landfill, advised people to hold on to their trash, and called for a fire ban—no barbecues or off-highway recreational vehicles. Although she announced the fire had grown to twenty-six hundred hectares, there were no more evacuations. She gave only a tinge of bad news, dipped in her sugary style: "This lovely, sunshiny weather can bring with it winds that can change."

Reading between the lines, I realized that the mayor was referring to the inversion effect. The coolness of the morning had pushed smoke to the ground with warm air crusting over it. That's why there weren't smoke columns over the trees like the night before. But when the day warmed as forecasted—to thirty-two degrees Celsius, a record high for May 3, with only 15 percent humidity—the inversion could pop like a pressure-cooker lid, lifting wind and the smouldering flames skywards. The wind had already shifted directions. The only missing ingredient for a firestorm was a faster current, and the more trees that burned down, the more surface area there was available for the wind to accelerate.

Blake gave the microphone to Fire Chief Darby Allen. "Last night was a classic situation," he said. "Everyone would have seen out their windows at eight thirty p.m. a raging fire, then, we wake up this morning and don't see anything. And people think it's fine, and it's all gone away. It's nice to have that thought, but I want people to bear in mind: don't get a false sense of security. We're in for a rough day. And it will wake up. And it will come back."

It would be four days before the fire would be nicknamed the Beast, but he obviously saw a monster from the maps and weather reports in front of him. There was a stark contrast between his ominous tone and the mayor's cheeriness. I was more discomforted, however, by Bernie Schmitte from Alberta Forestry, who delivered an omen with the matter-of-factness of a military bulletin: "At the time, there is a five-hectare spot fire that has crossed the Athabasca River."

I'd just dragged the garden hose onto the lawn when the first speckle of ash landed on the back of my hand. I was so focused on landscaping I hadn't noticed the warm wind on my face—blowing east. The DJ claimed the winds had hit forty kilometres per hour—too fast for any dozer guards or ground crews to stop the inferno from spreading, I realized.

No way I could stay at home. I tapped my phone's home-screen button and it filled with texts from Mom and friends looking for answers. The most recent notification was an email from Good Shepherd School. They were evacuating the kids. The fire was near.

I called the battalion chief on duty that day, Kelly Golosky. "Hey, Golosky," I said, staring at the rising plumes, "things are looking bad. I better come in."

He hemmed and hawed. It's his job to be concerned about overtime and budget lines.

"Okay," he said. "Grab your stuff and get down to Fire Hall 1." There, said Golosky, he'd direct me to Thickwood Golf Course, where a ground crew had been battling hot spots the size of campfires. The spot fires were too frequent, and they needed more bodies. I'd have to grab my gear from hall 5 first, I told him.

The road to 5 was clear. No gridlock, no panic, but it wouldn't be long. In the truck, I listened to 93.3 Country's DJ read a press release from the Regional Municipality of Wood Buffalo: "Abasand, Beacon Hill and Thickwood neighbourhoods south of Thickwood Drive and between Real Martin Drive and Thicket Drive are on a voluntary evacuation notice," he said. "Residents should prepare for a mandatory evacuation within a thirty-minute notice.

Residents should evacuate to MacDonald Island Park." How we planned to squeeze a third of the city's population into a rec centre—granted, Canada's largest—was beyond me, but the operative word was *voluntary*. Even the schools' decisions to evacuate weren't mandatory.

Inch by inch, as the bay door rose to the rafters, I saw a kaleidoscope of grey, yellow and red plumes—clouds stuffed with flames—across the western edge, casting an ominous shadow over the entire city. The highway ahead was jammed with cars.

When I walked into the bay, it felt eerily hollow. B-Shift was nowhere in sight, and gone were all but three trucks: a red tanker with a portable water supply and two Smeal fire trucks. Upstairs, REOC must have been a flurry of activity, but downstairs I was alone. Or so I thought. I got changed into my navy blue uniform and walked out to grab my bunker gear.

"Damian," someone hollered from across the bay. It was Captain Jed Antony, calling me from over the tanker roof as he climbed into the driver's side. "Are you here on your own?" Adrenaline and urgency laced his question. "They sent me to bring this to the golf course."

"That bad, eh? Should I get in with—"

"No," he interrupted. "We just got a report that the fire has crested into Beacon Hill. I'm on my way there now. Not sure what you're doing, but there's a pump here ready to go." The door descended behind him, closing the view on what still seemed to be a manageable situation. I looked across the bay at Pumper 310, and without hesitation, I shoved my bunker gear onto the passenger seat, turned on the ignition and pressed the remote-control door opener.

Inch by inch, as the bay door rose to the rafters, I saw a kaleidoscope of grey, yellow and red plumes—clouds stuffed with flames—across the western edge, casting an ominous shadow over the entire city. The highway ahead was jammed with cars. Only seven minutes had passed. What would happen in seven more?

PART TWO

RAINING EMBERS

CHAPTER 4

THE BATTLE BEGINS

E veryone in Fort McMurray on May 3, 2016, has a tale about where they stood and what they were doing when the inversion broke between noon and one o'clock, releasing the flames from a trap of cool air into the sky.

Aidan sat in his Grade 3 science class when an announcement overhead interrupted the lesson on rocks and minerals: "Attention all students, please gather your jackets and belongings and prepare to evacuate. Stay in your classes. We're notifying all parents and guardians to pick you up." Aidan sat there, quiet, tense, wanting to comfort Taya on the other side of the school, and wishing he was with me in a fire truck—not to fight the flames, but because it made him feel safe.

Melanie pushed an overflowing shopping cart out of Save-On-Foods when the fire tore down Beacon Hill towards the kids. Any other time, driving to Good Shepherd School is ten minutes, but it took the same length of time just to get to the main road from the parking lot. She repeatedly called our neighbour Pam Garbin for help. When they finally connected, Pam said students had been shuttled to a shelter downtown at another school—right across the road from the grocery store. Melanie jumped the median strip in her Ford Escape and circled back for them, but there was a miscommunication. Pam had Aidan and Taya and they were en route to Saprae Creek.

Mom spent the morning volunteering for the lunch program at my niece and nephew's school, and the sky was blue when she arrived at Safeway for her cashier shift. Within the hour, every aisle from deli to bread had turned golden, and outside, a pillar of dark smoke eclipsed the sun. My sister, Danielle, called Mom in a frenzy. Danielle was trying to get to her kids, but the lanes were jammed. "If you're leaving town, get me, because I can't drive that highway by myself," said Mom. By then, most shoppers and staff had left, so she followed, rushed home to rescue my father's ashes, kept in his hunting bag, and waited for Danielle to get her.

These are just a handful of the eighty-eight thousand civilians who ran for their lives. As I drove Pumper 310 along the jammed city streets, I assumed I would regroup with my family and neighbours shortly. I had no idea that it would be weeks before I saw most of them again. The Brotherhood had to make sure there was something for them to come back to. Until then, some of the only faces I'd see belonged to the department's 152 members who stayed behind.

Trevor Shantz's eye exam had gone well enough, but the view outside the clinic cast doubt on the optometrist's results. In little more than an hour, the plumes on the other side of the city had risen high over the boreal forest, with red edges and a terrifyingly dark core. But the air was so hazy that he assumed it looked worse than it was. He drove home just as his roommate was leaving to play eighteen holes at the golf course in Thickwood, taking full advantage of the early warm weather. He made lunch, fed his pit bull–labrador, Hugo, and answered a phone call from his mom, who was 450 kilometres away in Edmonton visiting family.

"I'm seeing a lot of pictures on Facebook," she said. "Should we get over there and grab our stuff?"

"Stay where you are," said Shantz. "I'm going to work tonight anyway. I'll see what's going on."

Soon after he hung up, his roommate returned in a fluster. "We just got evacuated from the golf course," she said. "It's on fire."

"Watch my dog," he told her, running upstairs.

"Why?"

"'Cause I guess I'm goin' to work," he hollered from his bedroom as he scrambled for his uniform before driving to hall 4 in Timberlea. There, in the middle of gearing up, the tones sounded and the dispatcher called over the intercom: "All halls! All halls! Bring every apparatus and proceed to hall 1!"

Shantz group-texted his family: *You might not hear from me for a few hours. I'm going into work. This is a big one.* Everyone replied to say *stay safe* except for his sister, Sherianne. She was a little preoccupied at the moment, cruising down a bike trail in her SUV behind Trevor's brother-in-law Chris Relph, while an eight-week-old baby wailed in the rear-facing car seat behind her.

Relph had just been at hall 4 too, drying his sopping duty boots after having fought the fire the day before in TaigaNova, but he whipped back home to Abasand Heights as soon as he caught word of the evacuations. That two-kilometre drive took forty minutes, and as he finally neared the top of Abasand Drive, a long, steep hill wooded on both sides, two cops directing traffic away from the neighbourhood tapped on his window.

"We're not letting anyone in. You have to turn around."

"My wife and kids are at home. I have to get in and help them out," Relph said. The cops waved him through.

At home, where his fiancée gathered baby supplies in a frenzy, he packed the car with her bag, diapers and formula, and rushed in to grab precious valuables. He stopped and assessed the numerous pieces of hockey memorabilia worth tens of thousands of dollars, including an autographed and framed Team Canada jersey belonging to Carey Price, a goaltender he's tried—and failed—to explain the importance of to me on many occasions. But as the flames outside turned black from the artificial material catching fire, and Sherianne begged him to leave, he couldn't process everything of value and instead ran out with a painting of a giraffe from the nursery that he'd just bought in a silent auction benefitting our department brother Bo Cooper, who was battling leukemia. Relph directed his family through a walking path to the highway, now flanked by fire. Sherianne's windshield cracked from the heat, and flames licked the rims of her tires. All the while their newborn screamed in terror. Relph drove as quickly as he could to hall 1. He pulled into the already packed parking lot, flagged down a truck, grabbed his gear and jumped in. Lucky for Relph, the truck was headed to his neighbourhood. As they drove towards the fire, Relph felt ready to do a job he'd felt destined to work since he was a sixteen-year-old New Brunswick kid volunteering at his local fire hall.

While this was happening, Shantz was on a ladder truck driving to hall 1, a redbrick building nestled between the highway, a freeway and the Hangingstone River. Around him, he could sense the adrenaline in the speed-walking firefighters wearing bunker gear and civilian clothing, hurrying between the bay and a parking lot packed with personal vehicles, which greatly outnumbered the available fire and rescue trucks.

"Who's an operator?" called Battalion Chief Kelly. Shantz stepped into his view without hesitation, along with a handful of other firefighters who raised their hands. "Get down to Fire Hall 5. There are two pumps there. Bring them." The operators stepped into a fifteen-passenger squad van that peeled off and halted as soon as it hit the gridlocked freeway. The van was unmarked. There were no lights. Shantz, in the passenger seat, held his helmet on the roof while the driver honked, hoping evacuees would get the picture.

They weaved to hall 5, where only one of the two pumpers remained; I'd taken the other. Shantz eagerly jumped into the driver's seat of Pumper 311 with a crew of three other guys, and not a captain among them. They turned on the sirens en route to hall 1, but couldn't ignore a traffic fiasco on the corner of Gregoire Drive and McKenzie Boulevard, an important three-way intersection that had become an all-terrain road in the panic. Someone needed to man it. The boys jumped out of the truck and funnelled drivers south towards Airport Road, where they had a clearer path to the highway. Ten minutes later, an RCMP officer took over, but by then the fire was closer to them than hall 1—they could see it in Beacon Hill and Abasand on the west side of Highway 63, and across the road in Waterways, Fort McMurray's original neighbourhood, where the first rail station and fur-trading post once sat at the edge of Clearwater River. Just about any heritage left in this boom town lived there, along with 650 people in trailers and character homes.

Crossing the bridge into Waterways, Shantz kept his eyes on the flames flailing across Cliff Avenue, torching a block of the city's oldest houses, while desperately seeking an egress should the fire spread to the bridge and trap them. The last of the small neighbourhood's residents were passing them, going back the way Shantz came in. Through the smoke, Shantz spotted Captain Brad Harding, breathing through an air pack as he trekked to the hoses. "Brad," Shantz called through the window as he approached him. "We need a captain." Brad got into the cab and directed them to a hydrant near Polaris, an ATV shop. They connected their hand lines and ground monitors while Shantz distributed water and foam from the pumper, but it was a pitiful sight as the stream arcs fell short. Because of all the burnt-out houses across the entire neighbourhood, the hydrants were tapping out, giving bad flow and forcing firefighters to get nearer to fully involved homes. Overhead, a helicopter dropped a bucket of water that evaporated in a cloud before it touched the roofs.

The flames spread to a block of trailers by the Polaris, heating up their staging area so fast that guys leaped from the hose lines they were operating and ran to their truck with the nozzles gushing. Shantz turned off the water and backed the truck half a block, dragging the hoses, but the flames leaped onto the Polaris building, popping propane tanks like popcorn.

"Captain!" Shantz called, sticking his head out of the cab and squinting through the smoke. "Captain! We gotta go." Captain Harding was nowhere to be found. Another crew had absorbed him in the chaos.

A rescue truck rolled up with a different captain. "We're all leaving," the captain said. "Pack up whatever you can, and follow us."

Shantz's crew shut down the lines, closed the ports, threw the hoses onto Pumper 311 and ripped back to hall 1.

Early that afternoon, Tia Morari was packing a suitcase of clothes for herself and her sons for the next week. She had booked a doctor's appointment in Edmonton and had decided to spend a few extra days there with the boys. As she rolled the suitcase to the family's SUV, the orange haze creeping across her block stopped her in her tracks. Timberlea is on the far north side of town—it shouldn't have been that smoky, so she could tell that something had changed. That morning, she'd already thought about cancelling her scheduled time away and had called her mom in Saskatchewan, asking her to meet Tia in Edmonton to care for her kids, Briggs and Maddox, at least until the air quality improved. That way she could return home after the trip and work overtime in the bush. As the scent of burning timber filled her nostrils and watered her eyes, she was ready to cancel the appointment completely—just get the boys to Edmonton and get the hell back.

Tia left the suitcase in the driveway and knocked on her neighbours' door. They had two small girls, her sons' ages, and Tia worried about their safety. "Pack up your kids and go," she said. The other parents didn't need any more convincing—the urgency in Tia's voice spoke for itself.

She hurried inside and cased her house for photo albums and snacks for the boys. Still, she didn't think it was so bad that Charlie, their pit bull, would have to come too, as long as her husband, Steve, a firefighter with Suncor, was still in town. She filled Charlie's food and water bowls, scooped up three-year-old Briggs in her arms, took Maddox's hand and left.

As soon as she hit Confederation Way, she regretted leaving Charlie. The highway, which encircles the northwest portion of the city and connects it to Highway 63, was a car park. She called Scott Germain, a firefighter who lived nearby.

"Have you left the house?" she asked.

"On my way to hall 1. They want everyone there—everyone. Even industry. Where are you?"

She looked around. It was impossible to see a street sign among the gridlock. "I'm in the world's largest parking lot," she said. "I need you to get my dog. Please. Bring him to the hall. I'll tell Steve later, but I have to get my boys out."

"No problem," Scott said.

Tia gave him her garage codes and tightened her grip at the wheel. She turned to her boys. Briggs was in his little nylon police costume and Maddox was dressed as Iron Man. "Everything is going to be okay," she reassured them. "We're going to get you to Grandma in Edmonton. Mommy and Daddy will have to work, but there's nothing to be afraid of."

The boys were surprisingly calm, but Tia wasn't. When she reached the Steinhauer Bridge over the Athabasca, she caught an unobstructed view of the city and flames that, if not already in Beacon Hill, were only minutes away. She called another friend in Timberlea. Before her friend could say hello, Tia asked, with steely adrenaline, "Do you have room?"

"Why?" asked the friend.

"Do. You. Have. Room?"

They said they didn't; their vehicles were packed to the brim. Tia called another: "Please take my kids, please." And another: "Well, make room—I don't care." And another: "They don't need a car seat, just get my boys out of town." Nobody wanted to turn around.

Tia broke down and sobbed. "Mommy, I'm scared," Briggs cried.

"Where's Charlie?" asked Maddox.

"Charlie's safe," she said, choking on tears. "He's going to the fire hall with Daddy." Steve worked that day, and if Scott was right, he would have been called to hall 1 with everyone else on shift, private employees or not. But she couldn't abandon the Brotherhood, not that they would have judged her for it. She had no family here except Steve, and one parent's sacrifice was sacrifice enough. Still, Tia felt stuck between being a bad firefighter and being a bad mom.

She looked at her fuel gauge. Just under half a tank. It wouldn't get her far, but it would get her out of town.

Her phone buzzed. Was it a friend who'd changed their mind? No, it was Steve's mom in Saskatchewan, panicking about her grandkids. "Steve texted me and said the city is burning. Are you in Edmonton yet? Please say you got out."

Sobbing, Tia blurted, "I don't have enough gas."

Silence fell over the car. The kids stopped crying. She stopped crying. And all her mother-in-law heard was the honking of a thousand cars a thousand kilometres away.

Tia called Steve, who was indeed at hall 1, with four guys and a massive industry pumper, waiting for deployment. They'd already driven through Beacon Hill and witnessed houses on fire. "We're in for a long-term fight," he told Tia.

"I'm bringing the boys by the hall to say goodbye," she said.

"There's no time."

"What if you never see them again?" she yelled, regretting it immediately as she caught a glimpse of her boys in the rearview mirror. "Don't leave," she told Steve, as she manoeuvred through downtown traffic towards him.

Once there, she carried Briggs and pulled Maddox by her side. Her feet clapped the pavement in flip-flops as she scanned the parking lot for Steve. It would be hard to miss his pumper—a red bombadier-looking engine that's designed for airport rescues and military air bases, and could conquer any terrain. We call them ARFFs (Airport Rescue and Firefighting), or crash trucks, and there his was at the front of the line.

Steve crouched down and hugged the kids, but before his knees straightened Tia told him she was staying.

"You have to go," he said.

"This is a serious operation," she said. "I can't leave."

"Tia—"

"If anyone is staying, it's me!" she interrupted. They went back and forth, bickering about whose responsibility it was to protect the town, and whose responsibility it was to protect the kids.

"Well, what the hell are we supposed to do?" asked Steve. Over his shoulder, fire was barrelling down the hillside, coming into Grayling Terrace, on the other side of downtown.

"Gear up," said Dana Allen, the assistant deputy chief of medical, dropping a pair of extra-large coveralls and oversized boots by Tia's feet. Tia pulled them on—they were a little big, but she didn't care, she was going to be part of this fight—kissed her husband and brought the kids to the hall's front desk with their belongings. "I need you to look after my boys," she told the receptionist.

Charlie was already there. The boys yelped with joy and wrapped their arms around him as he licked their faces. Tia talked to the receptionist: "I'm going to call friends, everyone I can, to get them out of here and bring them to safety. But until then, please don't let them out of your sight."

Tia kneeled down to the kids' and dog's level. "Mommy and Daddy are going to work for a couple days, okay?" The boys, simply happy to have their dog, nodded calmly. "This lady is going to look after you, then one of Mommy and Daddy's friends . . . I don't know who yet . . . but one of our friends will come get you and take you . . . somewhere safe."

Tia turned to leave, but Maddox called back for her. "I want tools."

"What for, honey?"

"I wanna help Mommy work."

Tia smiled all the way to storage and all the way back, and she handed the boys hammers and extra fire helmets. She hugged and kissed them, then got on Pumper 311 just as Trevor Shantz and his embattled crew stepped off, looking shell-shocked. Captain Mark Pomeroy took over, firefighter Steve Morriseau took the wheel and they formed a crew that stuck together for the entirety of the blaze.

*B*OOFFF. A chunk of ash dropped on Joe Jamieson's condo balcony like a phone book from outer space, channeling an instant childhood memory of another massive thud—a size-twelve boot landing inches from his face.

He was eight then, on his back, bloodied and unconscious after knocking his head on a diving board attempting a front flip. A lifeguard pulled him to poolside, while a crowd of shivering swimmers formed around his nearly naked body, panicking as another pool of blood formed around his head. His eyes opened the moment help arrived in the form of a group of firefighters in heavy boots. They checked his vitals, bandaged his head and assured him he was going to be okay. As he rode with them in an ambulance, smitten by their kindness, he asked them what they were doing before coming to his rescue.

"Basketball," said one of the firefighters. "We were shooting basketball."

"That's so cool," said little Joe in his daze.

From that moment on he knew he'd become one of them, even saying so in his high school yearbook. But his application to firefighting college was rejected. Speaking to a captain, he asked what he could do about that. "Go get a trade," he advised. "We like guys who know their ways around tools." Jamieson did just that, working as a plumber in his hometown, Kitchener, Ontario, for several years, until finally going to fire school. Because of that first career, his understanding of structure fires had been perfected, and his work ethic as an apprentice made him a workhorse. But more than anything, he retained his firefighting instincts—the kind of confidence that sends an eight-year-old flipping off a diving board. And the moment he saw the smouldering block of charred wood on his balcony, those instincts came rushing back to him.

He called his mom in Ontario. "I'll be careful," he promised her. "These are some of the best firefighters in Canada. We'll protect each other."

"Be safe," she cried.

"They train us that way."

"Call every day."

"I'll try."

"Promise me, Joe," she begged.

"I promise. Every day, I'll call," he said, grabbing his gear and leaving. He forwent the elevator, running down four flights of stairs and into the outdoor parking lot. The residential streets in Eagle Ridge, a subdivision of Timberlea, were clogged all the way to Confederation Way and beyond. He left his car behind and ran four hundred metres across the freeway to Fire Hall 4, where a ladder truck rolled out just as he arrived. They slowed for him to get in, but the cab looked like an overcrowded elevator. "I'll find my way there," he said, waving them on. He paced around the halls, looking for another truck to jump on, but the ladder was the last.

"We're taking our personal vehicles to Beacon Hill," one colleague told him.

"Good luck with that," replied Jamieson dismissively. He ran next door to the RCMP office and hopped in a police pickup en route to Abasand Heights, off-roading on lawns and sidewalks to get across the bridge. The panic was setting in. People were losing their minds, crashing into each other and running down the roads alongside deer galloping away from the flames.

Once in Abasand, Jamieson jumped out of the truck and started clearing houses with the police, ambulance and other emergency personnel practically putting their fists through the doors they banged on. Abasand is a subdivision that's mainly composed of apartments and row houses, so if one roof caught fire, dozens of people would lose their homes at once. Joe panned the area to make sure every driveway was clear or, at least, was about to be, but he stopped at the sight of an old man bawling on the stoop of a row house on fire.

"What are you doing? Go!" Jamieson yelled, marching towards the old man. "Now's not the time to cry."

"There are kids inside this house," he sobbed.

"What?"

"There's a woman in there with her kids. I can't leave till they're out."

"How do you know?"

"I'm their neighbour. I haven't seen them leave."

Joe gazed up at the roof. The fire on the other end was snaking inside through the eavestroughs.

"Are you one hundred percent?"

"I'm one hundred percent."

Jamieson shook his head and tried the door handle. It was locked. "Step aside," he said. He reeled back his leg and booted the door open, knocking it half off its hinges. A woman sat on the couch with two scared toddlers, staring blankly out the window. She was in utter shock. "Ma'am, do you not see what's going on here?"

She turned to him, steel-like. "We're not leaving."

Jamieson had to give his head a shake. "Ma'am. This townhouse is on fire. Your house. Is on fire."

"I'm not going anywhere," she said coolly.

"Here's the deal," he said. "If you're going to stay, I'm taking your kids and getting them to safety."

"You can't take my kids."

"I *will* take your kids and I *will* give them to the RCMP."

The mother wouldn't budge. Jamieson stood there in the doorway, smoke wafting in from behind him, and engaged in a brief staring contest with her. Then he snapped forwards, scooped a boy in his left arm and a girl in his right. He started leaving with them, pausing only to look back, in disbelief, at the woman sitting on her ass. He shook his head and marched to an RCMP officer outside, while the toddlers screamed and punched at his back. "Tell that woman she's got to leave," he said, then swiftly turned to the old man. "Listen, man, what I'm about to do is completely wrong, but can you take these kids and go with the RCMP out of town?" The man nodded dutifully, took the kids and sat them in his truck.

Jamieson returned to see how the police were making out. A haggard man stumbled down the stairs, rubbing his eyes. "Sir," said the officer and Joe in tandem. Joe continued, "You and your wife have got about three minutes till your house burns down."

The man belched. "I guess I'll go find my keys, then," he said, annoyed by the inconvenience. He sauntered around the main floor, checking in pockets of strewn pants and jackets, behind cups and under magazines. As he started back up the stairs, Joe chased after him, beating him to the filthy bedroom and finding the keys himself, all while the roof could collapse on him at any moment. The officer dragged the woman out while she screamed, and Jamieson pushed the man to his car, opened the driver's side, shoved him inside, threw the keys at him and slammed the door. The old man returned with the kids and they drove away just as fire entered their bedroom.

A lifted Dodge barrelled towards Joe through a soccer field like a getaway car, knocking into a fence of another house on fire. Kyle Leonard, a colleague from the department, stepped out of the driver's side while cops screamed at him to turn around and leave. "I'm going to my fucking house," he yelled back.

"You don't have time," a cop shouted over the flapping flames and sirens.

"Don't tell me what I have time for."

Jamieson had to intervene. "He works with me, let him do what he's gotta do," he said. "Leonard, what'dya need?"

"I don't know," he said in a huff. "Just let me get my bike out."

They lowered the ramp of his truck, ducked under flames hanging off the eavestroughs, lifted the garage door and rolled his Harley into the back of his Dodge. "Godspeed," said Jamieson.

By now, almost every house on the block was in flames. Joe and the officers and medics evacuating houses were choking on black fumes. Joe tore off his duty shirt and wrapped it around his face.

It resembled a war zone. Choppers and tankers zoomed above. Sirens wailed across the landscape. An apartment parkade was backed up, and drivers were screaming for help because they were pinned under the building. People abandoned their vehicles in the gridlock, running with their dogs and kids towards the highway. Joe yelled at them to go to Mac Island, an hour's trek at the best of times. "I can barely walk," pleaded an old lady, clutching a rolling suitcase and wearing glaucoma sunglasses. "I won't make it on foot."

"I'm sorry," he said, rubbing smoke out of his eyes. "I don't know what to tell you. You are going to have to walk." He looked like he was crying as he said it, but it was the fumes stinging his eyes. The old lady removed her hulking sunglasses and put them on his face, touched his cheek gently, thanked him for his service and rolled her suitcase towards the highway.

A police cruiser stopped beside him. An officer opened the passenger door. "We're getting out of here," she said. "Get in."

"You're not leaving," Jamieson tried to order them. "Look how many people are still here."

"It's not safe," she said. "You need to leave."

"No way," said Jamieson.

"Suit yourself." She shut the door and peeled off into the soccer field, followed by three more police vehicles.

"That's a little different," Joe muttered under the shirt around his face as he continued to help people into their cars, or out of their cars. Just out of this hell.

The smoke was suffocating, and he was dizzy, staggering around a crescent, holding himself up on the walls of houses he was checking for civilians. All he could see now were two blinking lights in the smoke, crawling across the front lawns. They stopped, and Captain Adam Bugden emerged from the smoke in a red helmet and bunker pants. He grabbed Jamieson forcefully, holding him up in his arms. "The hell are you doing?"

"I need a BA," gasped Jamieson. Bugden threw Jamieson's arm over his shoulder, dragged him to the truck and sat him on the bumper by the backup breathing apparatus kept in a side cabinet. He masked Joe, whose heavy gasping lightened with every inhalation, until he was ready to work again.

CHAPTER 5

"EMERGENCY TRAFFIC, EMERGENCY TRAFFIC"

F lames taller than Big Ben clock tower loomed above me in Beacon Hill as I finished opening the hydrant valve. I was the lone firefighter on scene, but I wasn't alone. On my way in, I thought there were going to be trucks everywhere. But that wasn't the case. I didn't see anyone else, but I could hear them on the radio, so I knew they were there. I didn't know if this was the best spot for me, but the fire was moving into the houses, so this was where I was going to make my stand. Across a block of bungalows, around side roads circling the 1970s cul-de-sacs, Fort McMurrayites ran to and from their driveways, loading boxes, pet kennels, kids. Far too many stood on their front lawns, pointing and talking as if the sky was an iMax theatre screen and not a sea of three-hundred-foot-tall flames hurling embers and burning flakes at them. I wanted to scream: *Get out! Go now!* But no one would hear me over the sirens from surrounding streets, the roaring fire and, loudest of all, the cannon of water blasting the trees blazing at their canopies. And there was so much smoke they couldn't see that houses were already hit.

When the ember smashed through the living room window in front of me, the flames lit up the vinyl siding and crawled up the side of the house faster than a squirrel up a tree. Then the fire snuck into the eaves, and into the attic and roof, engulfing their lightweight and open designs in a matter of seconds. The wind didn't have to stretch the flames far to catch the next vinyl siding eight feet away, and on they would travel from one house to the next like a door-to-door salesman of destruction if I didn't take care of them.

I needed to soak the houses, but the motor for the truck monitor—a mounted nozzle for pushing "big water"—was pooched and only shot in one direction. I'd have to use a small Allen key to change the nozzle direction—a daunting task, but a necessary one. Dashing between hydrant and cab, flipping switches and levers, shouting at folks to evacuate immediately, I worked every job of my fifteen-year career at once. I was a firefighter stretching water lines as far as possible, an operator controlling water and foam pressure from the cab, a captain pushing my own limits. And I was a probie, because whether you've been on the job for three weeks or three decades, no training, no drill and absolutely no manual can prepare you for your city on fire.

Training Officer Kratochvil's pickup finally tracked me down. Ten bodies jumped out of the truck bed, but I only recognized two of them: Matthew Heikel and Christine Pellegrin, both paramedics working towards firefighting certificates. In other words, not probies but a bunch of rookies in new uniforms and safety goggles without a mark on them who'd never seen a wildfire, let alone a structure fire, in their lives.

> Dashing between hydrant and cab, flipping switches and levers, shouting at folks to evacuate immediately, I worked every job of my fifteen-year career at once.

Heikel, a slim kid with an old cowboy moustache, grabbed a ground monitor for the first time in his life, and Pellegrin sat on the hose line to keep it to the ground, waiting for the line to charge. Only it didn't. Heikel fiddled with it until, suddenly, the water burst—right into their faces, soaking his moustache and Pellegrin's hair. "Spray it in the trees!" someone shouted at him. "Spray it at the house!" yelled another. "Spray it at the trees and the house," I corrected. "Hit it hard and hit it fast, get ahead—offensive attack."

"Hey, Cap, how's it going?" said a voice in the smoke. I turned to see Kyle Hitchcock in his soot-stained coveralls, walking towards me through the smoke like an apparition. He was nonchalant, with an air of coolness that said he was even more relieved to see me than I was to see him.

"A little busy," I told him.

"I'm here, what'dya need?"

"An operator."

"I'm your guy," he said, stepping into the cab. I put my hand against his chest.

"No," I said, fishing in my pocket and pulling out the Allen key. I handed it to Hitchcock. He took one look at it and knew what needed to be done.

He looked to the monitor, the arch of flames eighty feet overtop the truck reflected in his eyes. He shrugged, said "Okay," climbed the ladder, poked the crank with the key and twisted it left and right. The stream fell like a waterfall from midair on the houses and then onto the trees.

The probies finally got a handle on the hose, rotating it from trees to structures, back and forth, trying to slow the fire and guard the property. At the least, soaking people's homes made true believers out of skeptics, putting much-needed pressure on those still in houses that it was time to leave. Cars and trucks exited Beacon Hill Drive on both sides of me. In theory it was a sunny afternoon, and the day should have been clear as glass, but the thick plumes had eclipsed the sun.

It was time to turn my attention to the other probies around the truck, and to make sure everyone was out of the houses. "Grab piss-packs and hand tools. Work in twos, knock on every door and clear every residence. There are going to be embers everywhere—do what you can to put them out before they start the houses on fire." They pounded on the doors like crazed trick-or-treaters, yelling and banging, ordering residents to leave. Two of them emerged from one house with an armload of puppies. "What do you do with these?" they asked Kratochvil. He placed them gently in the back of his pickup.

Winds sped up, spraying as much water back at us as there was blasting into the trees. I was sopping wet, but my skin welcomed the coolant amid the hellish heat. I stepped into the truck, witnessing through the open side doors the flames running for the edge of the woods.

As I watched the pairs move further down the street, I stopped in my tracks and mumbled to myself, "How many did I send in?" We keep track of our crew on every call in case we have to pull out. We can't ever leave anyone behind. But this wasn't my usual crew, so I never got a head count. I hoped we wouldn't be ordered to leave.

The trees off-gassed blue hues and heart leaves singed as the fire built momentum with a startling roar. Heikel's and Pellegrin's heads snapped back to the tree line, mesmerized by a crush of flames sprinting at them through the canopies—then slamming into an invisible force field when it hit the road. Our sopping uniforms dried in an instant. The flames arched over Beacon Hill Drive, a deadly rainbow sending a blizzard of coin-sized embers at the houses. "Piss-packs, shovels, get hot spots," I ordered.

Hot spots are easy to extinguish. You can stomp them out. You can dump a bucket of water. But in this particular scenario we'd need ten thousand boots and buckets. We could not fight this like a traditional fire. I yelled, "Pellegrin, Heikel, hit them with water, soak the lawns!"

Barbecue propane tanks went off every twenty seconds. Then the fire got into the gun safes—*pop! pop! pop!* You could tell who'd been there longer by whether they flinched at the shots anymore. But we all shook when a massive boom on the other end of Beacon Hill Drive erupted—it was the end of the gas station I had passed coming in. "This sounds like Kabul!" shouted one member, an ex-soldier.

As the fire devoured more houses, it was beginning to feel as if we were working in a dark room—the only light source was the red embers flying across the air and fire around us. For the evacuees, getting out was like driving through Mordor.

Three trucks at a dead-end road in Abasand were trying to get caught up with the blaze, but every time their truck monitor hit the fully involved houses, the weakened roofs collapsed from the water pressure. Captain Adam Bugden, with Jamieson and an ever-growing crew, watched dumfounded as a fuse broke in one house and created an effect like an electrical storm inside. It didn't stop one civilian, a young man, from running back into his garage from his driveway. "What the hell are you doing?" yelled Bugden, chasing after him.

"Can I just grab something?" pleaded the man.

"You're going to die! You could die. Get out!" said the captain.

"I just need—"

"What part of 'get out' do you not understand?" Not two minutes after the man complied, a propane tank exploded inside the garage.

Captain Matt Collins shouldered up to Bugden as he sprayed a bungalow that had just caught fire. "We need you to protect the radio tower."

Bugden turned around, looking at the tower hundreds of metres behind him, in a protected zone nowhere near the flames. "That?" he asked in disbelief. He shook his head. "No, I'm not losing this house. We'll stop it here. If the time comes, we'll set up over there." He stood his ground, blasting the block in his bunker gear, but not everyone was so lucky to have had their protective gear on them.

Jamieson was huddled behind the truck, his skin almost bubbling. "Cap, I don't want to be the guy to ask, but can we go?"

"We still have water," said Bugden. He didn't just mean that they could protect the houses with it, but also themselves, should it come down to soaking personnel. As hydrants started giving out, however, he couldn't promise that much longer. He called for tanker shuttles to pick up the slack, but fifteen minutes later they hadn't arrived, and the hoses were dry.

It was the same sad story across Abasand. Relph was working out of a pickup truck with Mark Stephenson, Kyle Leonard—who returned after saving his Harley—and Darcy Sabey, alongside Captain Mark Pomeroy's crew in Pumper 311. They checked every hydrant, getting farther and farther from the flames, but each one was dry. "Emergency traffic, emergency traffic, emergency traffic!" radioed Captain Collins. When you hear that code three times, it means shut up and listen. "Abasand crews gather at a muster point, Athabasca Avenue and Abasand Drive." Without hesitation, they broke down their lines and readied to leave.

Morari tossed a forty-five-millimetre yellow attack line in the cab and was just about to get in when she noticed two hoses stretched into the engulfed crescent she had just left. A sickening feeling spread through her gut. She looked into the cab; Keegan Thomas wasn't there. The last time she had seen him, he was inside the crescent with Sabey. "I went there with two guys," she said to Jerron Hawley. "Where are they?"

A one-second pause felt like a year, but then it exploded as she and Hawley pulled air packs onto their backs and masks onto their faces in record-setting time. They sprinted into the black smoke, just as Thomas and Sabey staggered out—no bunker gear, no BA, no goggles, not even an N95—hacking and heaving under the coveralls pulled over their faces. Morari and Hawley pulled Thomas into the cab, Pomeroy did a head count and they sped away, leaving those two lines for the fire to swallow.

Slowly and steadily, I took control of the block on Beacon Hill, and the more I did it, the larger my crew grew. The probies clung to the calm, consistent direction I was offering. But the air quality was awful, as more houses caught on fire and the smoke thickened, and it was getting uncomfortably hot. Everyone was back at the truck and the block was reported clear—everyone was out of the houses. The fire in the trees at our location was mostly out, but the fire was starting to push through the houses. We needed to move in further.

I ordered the probies to disconnect the hoses, wrap them up and move down the street. Heikel and Pellegrin jumped on with me, as well as two other probies who crammed in the back with them, and Hitchcock took the wheel. "When did you guys graduate?" I asked.

"Uhh," mumbled Brian, "supposed to be next month." Their training was only 90 percent complete.

We rolled through black smoke and panicked evacuees who were jumping curbs, front lawns and ditches in their pickups. City folk love to mock us for our love of big trucks, but never was there a better justification for the town's manly motorcade than the evacuation of an entire populace over so few roads.

Houses caught fire in Beaver Lodge Close, a cul-de-sac off the main drive. It was our next stop, even though we risked getting trapped inside if the route in was choked off. "Clear the streets," I commanded. "Make sure there's no one left in their houses." Pinching their shirts over their mouths and noses, the probies banged on every one of the doors, practically putting their fists through them. Heikel and Pellegrin hit one, another pair hit the next, and then Heikel and Pellegrin leapfrogged them. *Bang! Bang! Bang!* If it was locked and no one answered, they'd run off, sprinting clockwise around the crescent in steel-toe boots.

As they evacuated the block, I dragged the ground monitor to one backyard, pointing it towards the strip of trees on the other side of the crescent. Just about every one of our neighbourhoods connects to an urban parkland—a lifestyle luxury on any day but today. Erratic winds shifted east, then north, then west. Jogging to the truck, my feet squished around in my sopping boots, like I was crushing tomatoes with every step.

The radio squawked with more reports of areas under attack: "We're in Waterways, houses on fire!" "Tanker to Abasand!" "We've lost water supply!" "We can't find our way out." It all blended together, a melody of turmoil and adrenaline, until I heard the call, "Emergency traffic, emergency traffic, emergency traffic! Abandon Beacon Hill. The fire is over our heads. Drop your lines and leave the area."

I punched the ceiling. I still had people in houses. I still had a water supply. I still had men and women soaking houses. I couldn't leave yet, not until I was sure everyone was out and every single house had been checked.

The fire trucks funneled into an Esso parking lot at the top of Abasand Drive. The captains strategized under the fuel dispenser awnings while firefighters gathered in a small crowd by three trucks and a couple of fleets. Tia, Chris and Joe stood together. "Where's your family?" Joe asked Chris.

"I sent them down a bike trail," he said.

"You're kidding."

Chris didn't reply; he just watched the captains in silence and waited for the next order. Captain Collins was commanding the area, speaking quietly with Captains Bugden and Pomeroy. What they were talking about was on everyone's mind—everyone wanted to go back in. After five minutes, the officers made their way to the firefighters.

"We're going back in," said Collins. "Tankers are coming, and they're going to follow us in."

"We're going back to where we were," Bugden said to his men. "Set up and do water suppression."

The first tanker on a semi truck pulled up Abasand Drive, and the firefighters hopped back into their cabs and seats. But the roads were too smoky and the tanker didn't see them. It just rolled through the intersection, into the black smoke. The captains tried the radio, but their call was breaking up. The fire had reached the tower, compromising communications. Captain Collins went after it in a squad truck, and the next time the radio signal worked it was his voice: "Emergency traffic, emergency traffic, emergency traffic—we're abandoning Abasand."

"Goddamn Carey Price jersey," Relph mumbled under his breath as he pulled the seat belt on. One by one, the trucks pulled away from the gas station and drove slowly down the smoking hill.

In Pumper 311, Morriseau focused on what little road he could see in front of him, and Captain Pomeroy turned to Morari and the others. He placed his helmet back on his head and cleared his throat.

"Listen," he said. "I'm going to take you guys through some hairy situations today. You may not agree. But you need to trust me. It might not make sense, but you have to remain strong. We're here to fight the fire."

Melanie was trying to get to our campsite in Boyle, three hundred kilometres south, where she and the kids planned to stay in the camper until things blew over, as they had the year before. When Melanie had got the kids home earlier that afternoon, she'd still thought it was a standard evacuation. "Pack some clothes for the week," she told them, then folded a few changes of clothes for herself and me. Taya tried to pack twenty pairs of socks along with her giant stuffed hippo. "That's ridiculous," Melanie said. "You'll only need two pairs." The hippo could stay, though. Aidan brought along his baby blankie, which, after nine years, he still couldn't part with. But as she commanded the kids, tried to coerce the dog and two skittish cats into kennels, unpacked the groceries she had just bought and fielded a flurry of text messages from her family, my family and every friend assuming that she—as a fire captain's wife—would have fire updates, Melanie lost track of where she'd put her phone. It took her forty-five minutes to find it in her yoga bag, of all places, and when she finally retrieved it, it was clear that there was nothing standard about the evacuation anymore.

I told her to fill up her Nissan Armada with the jerry cans of gas in the garage and hit the highway soon as she could, even if Saprae Creek hadn't received an evacuation notice yet. That should keep her going for a few hours—about as long as she'd spend lined up at a pump, if there was even a drop left in town. I checked in with her on and off.

How are you doing?

Frustrated
They are making ppl turn around
The ac isn't working bc it's so hot
The dog is losing her mind
They have to let us out don't they??

They have to just hold

It was the best I could offer her. I pocketed the phone and tried to command loud enough for my crew to hear: "Hook up to a hydrant. Gotta get a water supply. Stretch out a cross-lay to that side, a cross-lay over there. Stay one house back—use the hose stream to your advantage. Prepare for embers landing. Watch for hot spots." They could only follow half my orders. It was a clusterfuck, a bunch of youngsters bumping into each other, tying their hoses into knots as they crisscrossed the cul-de-sac. Any other day, they'd all have been on the bumper by now. But I needed them and I had to keep it together—as a firefighter, your emotional state is infectious, and it starts at the top. You let your emotions take control and things spiral fast.

> "Prepare for embers landing. Watch for hot spots."

Once on the ground, I regained order. I ran up to Tyson, grabbed him by the straps of his piss-pack and pushed him towards an alley. "I want you to cover the back. You—" I said to Heikel, so loudly that his moustache rustled in my breath, "I want you down here." I pushed him towards a bike trail with a hose and shovel.

Dim orange headlights creeped towards us through the smoke. An officer I didn't know stepped out of the bed, where a tank of water swished around, and walked right past me. I glimpsed a green triangular patch, the logo of the Town of Slave Lake, on his shoulder.

Earlier that week, REOC had requested firefighters from Slave Lake, a town 440 kilometres away, needing their expertise. In 2011, a wildfire had razed a quarter of the town, leaving a swath of the seven thousand residents homeless. It was the costliest natural disaster and the largest evacuation in Alberta history until that afternoon, when Slave Lake firefighters found themselves hauled into Fire Hall 1 and sent back out to a familiar scene. Hitchcock had jumped into one of their fleet trucks, but sometime between then and now he went MIA.

"Hey," the Slave Lake captain barked at Hitchcock. "Don't ever just jump out and abandon me. We're a crew now. Even if it's only been twenty minutes, we're a goddamn crew." Little did I know that Hitchcock hadn't relayed to the officer that he was staying with me to operate my truck—I didn't have an operator and desperately needed his help.

In any other scenario, I'd have ordered Kyle to go back to his original crew.

"Listen," I told the officer. "Hitchcock is one of my men and has been since the day he stepped on the floor." I pointed over his shoulder to the tank in his truck. "That a sprinkler trailer?" In the truck bed sat big garden sprinklers that we could stick in the ground to cover a hundred-foot radius. "Think you can park in the alley, set it up along the tree line and moisten them?" I had to frame it as a question, so as not to piss him off any more. He shook my hand and did it.

B y early evening, Fire Hall 1 was an animal house, with a doggy daycare growing in one room and two horses neighing in the bay.

The stranded firefighters and EMTs were desperate to get on trucks returning from Abasand, but the Abasand captains were not desperate for relief. Instead they came to re-rack hoses and resupply after losing equipment and to pool resources.

"Shantzy," Jamieson called across the bay, noticing Trevor sitting alone. "Where's your truck?"

"I don't have one," he said.

"Well, get in with us."

Shantz jumped to his feet and hurried to Pumper 320. "Where are we going?" he asked as he opened the cab to eleven guys packed like sardines, sitting on the pump panel, crouching on wet hoses. They pulled Shantz inside by his arms and took off.

Inside the hall, Morari was reassuring her boys that someone would come to get them soon. She still didn't have a clue who. "If you need to stay here with the kids . . ." Pomeroy asked her.

"No, I'm good," she said before he could finish his sentence. Morari didn't want to give up her spot on Pumper 311. Whether her crew thought it was right or wrong, they told her it was the right decision to keep her motivated, to stanch the guilt and to keep her from backing out. She kissed the boys one more time, not sure if she'd see them again in two hours, two days, or two weeks.

We had a hell of a fight in Beaver Lodge Close, saving what houses we could. Without proper firefighter gear, our skin was exposed to a blistering radiant heat, and there weren't enough respirators to keep us from choking on the fumes, but we were determined to stop the fire. "Damian," said Captain Antony, carrying an unhooked ground monitor with blackened sweat dripping from his forehead. "Everyone is leaving. I think we should too."

"What do you mean? We still have water, and there are still houses to be saved. Are all the residents out?"

"Everyone's out. You're the last truck in here."

"There's still work to be done."

"I know, but the fire is moving into Wood Buffalo. It's jumped the Athabasca. They're asking for everyone to move up to that location." I nodded, as he started shouting at guys to evacuate.

"Withdraw!" shouted another voice.

"Evacuate Beacon Hill."

"Drop everything and leave."

Heikel dropped the attack line and sprinted towards our pumper. "What the hell are you doing?" I asked.

"They said drop every—" he stuttered.

"We need that stuff. Pack it." I had a sense that if we didn't pick up our equipment, we'd regret it later.

Heikel rushed back, decoupled his hose, unscrewed the fittings, drained the hose, flanked it around his shoulder and tossed it into the back cab. Now we were on the move, with Hitchcock behind the wheel.

As we drifted through the carnage, I saw from the top of the hill an endless stream of dim red eyes in the smoke along the highway. I turned on the stereo, dialed it to 93.3: "The city of Fort McMurray is under a mandatory evacuation order," the DJ announced. "If you are south of Beacon Hill you should head to Anzac Recreation Centre. If you are north of downtown Fort McMurray, including downtown Fort McMurray, you should head north to Noralta staging point. If you are uncertain on directions just head north on 63 and follow the track directions from there. This radio station is unmanned. Do not call the radio station seeking assistance—" I jabbed my thumb into the dial to silence it.

I watched Beaver Lodge Close burn in the side-view mirror. I felt pangs of guilt about the houses that would have stood a chance had we stuck around, even though I knew that a single truck couldn't make that big a difference. But it just wasn't safe, and I had to protect my brothers and sisters, even if I didn't know half their names. Five or six guys—I lost count of how many people were jumping on my truck—were crammed in the cab with equipment, standing over one another with shell-shocked expressions, leaning on one another for balance and probably more. I could only hope no one was left behind, but it was impossible to keep track of the bodies on the ground, shuffling from truck to truck. "If you're on my truck," I said, "then you stay on my truck." I turned to Hitchcock, squinting to see through the smoke. "Take it slow."

Through the smoke, I could see the rest of the city on the other side of the Hangingstone River Valley. The fire had ripped through neighbourhoods so fast it had already jumped the highway, hurdling over cars as they evacuated. There was Abasand, up in smoke. Waterways, glowing red. The Super 8 motel and Denny's fell in on themselves, and a nearby road was covered in debris and closed down after the gas station exploded. It was almost quaint to think that the year before, when our department lost four houses on a block one night, we had felt it as an incredible loss. Now, twice the damage was happening on an hourly basis and would only get worse. I was ready for the fight of my life, but would the rookies on my truck have it in them?

Our cellphones simultaneously chimed. It was TeleStaff, an app used for mass messaging city staff, summoning all firefighters to the battle. I let out a brisk laugh. "Oh, I guess we better come to work. Apparently there's a problem." Then I turned to my guys with sincerity. "This will be all night long. Call loved ones, call whoever you've got, because we got about ten minutes till we get to the next battle."

CHAPTER 6

MAKING IT UP AS
WE GO ALONG

"You guys aren't trained for this!"

I had to hold the phone inches from my ear. It was Mom, shrieking from the passenger seat of Danielle's SUV, clutching Dad's ashes in her lap, while my sister followed her husband north.

"Just get to Fort McKay," I said. Fort McKay is the First Nations reserve sixty kilometres north of Fort McMurray. The furthest north you can go in Alberta without a plane, it's literally the end of the road. There was no reason to suspect the fire could spread that far and trap the community, so with the bulk of McMurrayites driving south towards Lac La Biche and Edmonton, I urged they avoid the gridlock and go the other way.

Mom seemed to be in a better situation than Melanie. It was too late for Melanie to turn north, so I kept reassuring her over the phone to stay put: "They have to let you go. Wait it out. Just keep trying." Getting from Airport Road to Highway 63, then to Highway 881—a narrow southeast road that curls around Gregoire Lake and Stony Mountain Provincial Park—took two hours instead of the regular twenty minutes, as her windshield wipers swiped at raining embers. Inching through smoky traffic, frying inside the car with broken air-conditioning and six dehydrated humans and animals, she wondered whether she'd packed the right necessities or whether the hard drive she'd snatched contained our beloved family photos or just downloaded cartoons (it was the movies). In that state of mind, who could blame her for not thinking to shut her car off as traffic stalled? She didn't notice the fuel gauge hand creeping backwards until it was too late. Luckily, our friend and neighbour Kelly was a few cars ahead. Melanie called her for help, and with traffic at a standstill, Kelly ran down the road yelling, "I need a jerry can," until she succeeded and fuelled Melanie's Armada.

I worried for the family, but I had to keep a firm grip on our battle. I had heard no strategy from dispatch in a while. Everything felt improvised. Judging from the fire's behaviour, shoving northwest, getting to Wood Buffalo Estates seemed smart. The neighbourhood is fifteen kilometres from Beacon Hill, on the other side of the Athabasca River that the fire had jumped. It was spreading at a rate of one kilometre per fifteen minutes, meaning it would reach the community within the hour.

Hitchcock steered us down the centre lane of Memorial Drive, flanked by panicked drivers, some of them awkwardly towing motorboats and fifth-wheel trailers that could have dragged them into the ditch. I commanded traffic over the loudspeaker: "Don't go south, go north! Follow us!" The northbound road at least wasn't gridlocked, and, though it also leads to a literal dead-end, there are dozens of industrial camps along the way capable of holding ten thousand people. "Turn north. Follow us," I repeated. Could they hear me through their closed windows keeping the smoke out, over the honking and sirens? I could barely make out my own words over the chatter from my crew talking to their loved ones.

"I'm safe—yes, it's very, very bad," I overheard one say to his mom.

"Did you get the bird?" asked another.

"Call your boss later, just move!"

Hitchcock called every friend to make sure they were all safe, including the ex-girlfriend he moved out here with from Ontario. "I can't hear you," he shouted, "but if you haven't left yet, you need to get out. Get your pets out. Get your cousins out. Go!" Not sure if they make World's Best Ex-boyfriend mugs but, man, does he deserve one.

Getting to the Wood Buffalo neighbourhood northwest of Beacon Hill was an ordeal. Developed during Fort McMurray's second oil boom on the north side of the Athabasca River, Wood Buffalo is a ten-minute drive on the best of days. But all along Memorial Drive and Thickwood Boulevard, two major roadways, people drove south through northbound lanes and north through southbound lanes, and they were immune to fire truck sirens after two hours of chaos. As frustrations mounted, drivers took leaps of faith through any open side road, not realizing that, as with almost every neighbourhood in this suburban-style city, there's only one way in and out of them all. I shook my head watching cars turn onto Timberline Drive, knowing they'd end up crawling through a U-shaped road back to Thickwood Boulevard, setting themselves behind and giving the fire a chance to gain on them.

The sight of the Fort McMurray Golf Course stunned me as we climbed the hill. Not because the green was black and the clubhouse was smouldering rubble, but because I shouldn't have seen it at all; the course is normally behind a thick fence of sixty-foot-tall trees. Conifers burn violently, sometimes in an effect known as candling. Fire grabs them by the trunk, creates a superheated gas ignition inside the trees like a backyard barbecue, and then after a brief crackle—*WHOOF!* Flames propel to the canopy and the tree disappears in seconds.

At the corner of Real Martin Drive and Wilson Drive, Captain

Ryan Pitchers's crew laid a seven-hundred-metre sprinkler line along a walking trail on the southeast edge of Wood Buffalo, between a cluster of condos and a greenbelt looking towards the golf course. If the sprinkler didn't stop the fire, there were ready crews scattered about the block, including volunteer firefighters from Anzac and Saprae Creek in Wilson Bay, spraying the houses that backed onto bushes, and Suncor in Woodward Bay with pumpers. Industry pumpers are decked out with dry chemical systems and remote-control nozzles, infrared cameras and up to fifteen hundred gallons of Class-A foam used to suppress large chemical fires. Wildfires are not their expertise, but they were there to help any way they could. We had a great line of defence between the city, industry and volunteer crews.

Hitchcock pulled Pumper 310 next to Pitchers's truck, Pumper 4, covered in an ashy skin. Three hours ago, it was on display outside a school, where Pitchers and his crew had been teaching kindergarteners about firefighting, marveling them with breathing apparatuses, cheerfully letting them wear his helmet. When he took them outside to see the main event, this shiny new Pierce, he found himself doing damage control instead. "Is that going to be a problem?" asked a teacher, staring at the glowing plumes.

"You better call their parents," he said, before texting his wife, Nancy, at the pet store they owned: *Shut it down. Send the staff home.*

Nancy booked it home—here in Wood Buffalo—to save their cats and hamsters. But their daughters, Kira and Alexandria, didn't get there. Instead, they were whisked away from their schools with a family friend. Their tight-knit family was split three ways: Nancy was driving south, the car with their girls was forced north, and Pitchers was here, a few blocks from his house, helpless to do anything for them.

I rolled down my window. "What's the deal?"

"Fire's down in the golf course," said Pitchers. "It's moving up the hill."

"Where do you need me?"

"Get down on Woodward Lane. You know the spot?"

Yes, I knew it well. It was the end of the road that Pitchers lived on. I had helped him purchase his roomy bungalow with an ornamental streetlight at the edge of an impeccably green lawn, and I assisted with the inspection and renovations that he did himself. He took a lot of pride in his home, and it showed. We set up on the elbow of Woodward Lane and started spraying in the bushes. Tons of deep forest surrounded us—an almost limitless supply of fire fuel—so if we didn't soak the timber, tinder-dry grass and the backs of houses, the fire could devour the area.

No flames were in sight, but a double-headed plume loomed over the northwest. Hitchcock became a de facto training officer by directing the crew to stretch hundreds of feet of fire hose and monitors all along the cul-de-sac, and leading by example.

"Come on," he teased a new firefighter, while lugging two rolls around his arms like heavy-duty hula hoops. "I'm pulling two, how come you're pulling one?"

While some were evacuating houses, others were now being trained as firefighters on the spot. Between a strip of Jack pines and houses, Kyle handed a paramedic a sixty-five-centimetre hose and directed another to hold the line behind him.

"What do I do with this?" asked the one in the front.

"You control the nozzle," he told her. He turned to the other. "You're the anchor. Take the nozzle reaction and try not to get knocked off your feet."

"Anything else?" asked the nozzle woman.

"Stand there and spray their trees."

"I can do that."

Hitchcock returned to the truck, cranked the levers and listened. You can diagnose pumper trucks by sound to know how hard the engine's working or whether water is flowing right. If the hydrant shits the bed and it takes in too much air, it'll make a godawful clunking sound, so a good operator knows to stay within earshot and never stray too far, because you might have to run back at a moment's notice. Each of Fort McMurray's six pumpers was a million-dollar responsibility.

The truck was fine, but we were getting minimal water supply. With so many hydrants operating at once and so many trucks on the same water loop, the pressure was abysmal. Thousands of people, rather smartly, had turned on their lawn sprinklers before getting out of Dodge. But as hundreds of houses in Beacon Hill, Abasand and Waterways collapsed under the fire, waterlines were snapping and draining unlimited water into the smouldering foundations. Nothing could stop the leaking, making the fight in Wood Buffalo akin to pissing on a bonfire—or at least it would once the fire touched down.

Hitchcock and I looked for leverage to extend our shots. A few residents hadn't left. "Do you have a ladder?" I asked a guy about to pull out of his driveway. He opened his garage with the remote control on his sun visor and invited me to take whatever we wanted. I thanked him as he drove away, and Hitchcock dragged an aluminum ladder to the side of the double garage. He directed a firefighter to climb it with a garden hose and sprinkler to spray down the house. It was a great decision—it meant we had one less spot to worry about—and I was once again reminded of how grateful I was to have Hitchcock by my side.

An ad hoc crew of probies and a training officer in a canopied pickup joined the fight, wetting the edge of the bushes to the west where the fire would come from. Together, we staged in that corner for eighty minutes, soaking it with millions of gallons of water, a perfect prophylactic against the inevitable. We helped swamp the southeast edge, but the fire didn't come. The wind was erratic, and without an aerial view, it was impossible to know how it was spreading. Intense heat and debris were creating different pockets of air currents ten blocks apart. A flag mounted on a manicured lawn changed directions, flapping intensely one way, then another, then another.

Battalion Chief Golosky got word that the fire had entered through a graveyard into JW Mann and was now blowing over Real Martin—the only road in and out of Wood Buffalo. Real Martin was gridlocked, as were the four tributaries to the one exit, narrow roads stuffed with bumper-to-bumper traffic trying to get out. "Be ready to abandon Wood Buffalo," Golosky said over the radio. We were still clearing houses.

"It's too soon," Pitchers radioed back. He was already adjacent to JW Mann, where an unspotted fire crested the hill and entered the subdivision with a sudden easterly wind change. The crescent fans into the bush, a pod of two-storey houses close together and backing onto dense fuel. The fire was blowing embers into adjacent streets and had started several house fires.

Pitchers radioed, "We have fire in the houses, and good water supply. People are still in the houses. We are holding here." Like Pitchers, I didn't want to prepare for abandonment either, but I trusted my battalion chief's judgment.

"We need an egress," I said into the radio. "Send them my way." I turned to Hitchcock. "Grab the hose, start wrapping up. Meet me by Ryan's house."

"Where?" he asked. I pointed seven houses north, sprinted to the other side of the truck, threw open a cabinet and grabbed a common chainsaw in practically one gesture, then ran up the block.

The remaining citizens in the neighbourhood were directed my way over loudspeakers by the ambulance crews assisting with clearing houses. "Follow us—we'll get you through. Follow the fire trucks to Woodward Lane." The other ground crews stood at the intersections, directing cars.

The bike trail was a shortcut to Thickwood, east of Wood Buffalo, except for a wood beam in the centre blocking all motorists from entering. Luckily, I knew a thing or two about wood beams. As I sawed the obstacle to a stub, a parade of personal vehicles followed Pumper 310: trucks pulling campers and trailers, private utility vans, campers and cars pulling speedboats and beds of off-road vehicles. The question of whether or not they could get through was answered by Pumper 310's narrowly squeezing across the path. The caravan followed me as I jogged two hundred metres with the chainsaw to decapitate the wood beam at the other end. Chainsaw packed, we led the motorcade through an off-leash dog park to Wolverine Drive so they could turn onto Thickwood Boulevard and get on the highway. A guy gunned it in an ATV, just having the time of his life, hooting and cheering for us as he passed the truck.

> Pitchers radioed to the department. "We're not abandoning this area," he said. "This is where we're going to make a stand."

Pitchers radioed to the department. "We're not abandoning this area," he said. "This is where we're going to make a stand." Other trucks had moved from their locations to assist Captain Pitchers in protecting the houses. The reports on the radio of trucks in place and water flowing made it sound as though the crews were winning against the fire.

We planned to loop right back over there to help, but as we cruised through Thickwood, we pulled a U-turn, turning back towards Ermine Crescent, where another plume was emerging from the bush.

The other volunteers and industrial firefighters in Wood Buffalo stayed behind and were redeployed to the western edge of Real Martin Drive. The fire was impinging on two apartment buildings by the time they got there, and then it caught hold of two houses at once and tore through the block, forcing the firefighters to move to a defensive attack.

The houses were so fully involved that they quit fighting the blazes and worked to save the other houses beside them, spraying their exposures. Otherwise, they'd be putting all their water on a lost cause, giving the fire a chance to spread to the next house, and the next, and soon they'd have conflagration—a firestorm like the one that swallowed the neigbourhoods we had had to abandon. Despite the soft water pressure, they managed to save most of the houses on JW Mann; however, much of the rest of Wood Buffalo resembled a suburb of Aleppo by the next morning. More than forty houses had burned to their foundations, leaving only charred playgrounds, bikes and barbecues as relics of the idyllic neighbourhood it once was. Almost 150 people were now homeless, but with our help and quick thinking, every one of them got out alive.

The pumpers of Captains Jeff Hamm and Adam Bugden were set up along Ermine Crescent to fight flames crawling out of the southeast tip of Thickwood, spraying the spruce forest with a massive wall of water while boots on the ground snaked hand lines in between houses, preparing for embers to land. "Give me a hand in Ermine Bay," Jeff told me.

We pulled into a cul-de-sac and ran hose lines behind seven bi-level houses butted up against a bush at the top of the hill, north of the golf course. The lines were stretched in pressure loops, in which one side of each hose holds down the other, and the firefighter straddles them as if riding a steer.

The sudden wind shift took everyone by surprise, so we were all working fast to knock down the flames. Heikel anxiously waited for Hitchcock to hook to the hydrant and fill his flaccid hose. A wall of fire picked up momentum and came right for us. "Give me water now, water now!" he yelled from the hose line. I knew the feeling— three seconds of anticipation that felt like thirty. But as quickly as he thought of running, the hose puffed up, and a stream of water rushed to him. He fanned a huge volume of water through the flames, cutting them off at the knees.

As the firefighters cooled the trees, a thousand-pound moose leaped out of the smoke, almost kicking one of them in the head as it galloped into the neighbourhood, which was filling with trucks now. Aside from rookie panic and the occasional near-fatal stampede, however, our adrenaline had tapered, and hunger was setting in. Hitchcock let the water flow and knocked on nearby doors, looking for remaining residents as a pretense for rummaging for food if the house was unlocked and empty. His hunt was unsuccessful. Dehydration worried me more. You can sweat three litres of water in a normal firefight, and this was far from normal. "If you're not pissing every hour," I said, handing every firefighter a bottle from the truck, "then you're not drinking enough water." The rescued litter of puppies from Beacon Hill panted and wept under the pickup canopy. Hitchcock filled a helmet for the animals to lap from, and soon every water bottle vanished.

There were some Gatorades on the truck too. Hitchcock loaded it all under his arms and started distributing it to the various crews. Shantz and Jamieson were sitting on the grass, hydrating themselves from a garden hose. Hitchcock appeared out of the smoke and lobbed a bottle at each of them. "Good to see all my friends aren't dead," he said, and then disappeared back into the smoke.

"What just happened?" Shantz asked Jamieson.

In Ermine Bay, we'd made the brush fire manageable. "You've got a lot of guys here," I told Captain Hamm. "We've done what we can. I'm roving around for embers."

"Good plan," he replied.

Pumper 310 crawled along Thickwood Boulevard, Wolverine Drive and Signal Road, and over the course of the night, drove a full circle around the entire northwest. "Everybody in the back," I said to my crew. "Everybody in the front," I said to Hitchcock and myself. "Have your head on a swivel. Look for any flames, any smoke. You see something—we'll hit it."

"There's one!" someone would shout, spotting a smouldering backyard or front porch to stomp out, a flaming shed or a fence to hose down. The crew was getting the hang of it, flying out of the cab with spades before Kyle had even stopped, and hooking up to hydrants speedily. There were brush fires that, on a normal day, would be considered 67-Delta—all hands on deck—though we were looking at them thinking, *They're just trees, move along.* But even limiting it to properties, at the rate that flying embers were terrorizing the vacated community, we had to go faster.

Moving is a pain in the ass once you're set up. Break down two-hundred-foot-long, four-inch hoses, each seventy pounds soaking wet, roll them up and toss them in the truck. Gather all tools, monitors, splitters—all back in the truck. Everything is meant to be tucked in a specific place like a Tetris block, but the way we were moving—stopping every few blocks to snuff out a hot spot—tools were disarrayed and crammed in the cab with the probies. Eventually, they didn't even bother to drop their shovels and pull off their piss-packs anymore, as we were stopping every few blocks to hit hot spots.

Setting up and striking was time-consuming, so I changed plans after the third stop. "Guys, forget the hoses and cross-lays. Forget the hydrant," I said. "Just use any garden hose you see. Turn it on, spray it out, get back over here soon as possible." After a while, we had a surplus of hand-nozzles, hoses and sprinklers, so that, if a house didn't have one, they could quickly connect whatever was on hand, leave the water running and go. No doubt this wouldn't help the strained water system, but it was still better than losing the house entirely to a fire.

It was mildly funny, seeing the crew jumping fences and scattering around the neighbourhoods like kids playing tag. "I've got a power nozzle. What do you got?" I overheard Pellegrin ask, all too gleefully.

"NeverKink right here," said another firefighter, referring to a premium garden hose that does exactly as its name suggests. "I need to get me one of these when I get home."

"Bro, dual-action wand? Somebody was living the good life."

Aside from not fighting an urban blaze with home products, policy would have advised we have full bunker gear and PPE—personal protective equipment—but the circumstances were such that we were doing what we needed to get ahead of the fire.

While Hitchcock drove and the firefighters extinguished hot spots (they'd graduated from probies to firefighters in this historic crash course, far as I was concerned), I listened to the spotty radio for updates: every emergency medical services and fire department apparatus was in use. A backup satellite was installed to keep cellphone communications from failing. The gas company was directed to shut down all gas lines into the city, lest one ignite with a house and blow a torch from the ground up. More apparatuses from across Alberta were en route, as was food and water from grocery stores that had given REOC permission to raid them. It must have been the world's best job to run through the isles of Safeway with a shopping cart, wiping groceries off the shelf with their arms like they'd won a supermarket sweepstake.

Downtown was mostly safe, but the fire jumped Highway 63 and embers lit a few houses near the hospital, causing a precarious evacuation of the sick. My colleague firefighter Anthony Hoffman and his crew had to guard it, setting a water perimeter on the ground with sprinklers. He dragged a standpipe-system hose from the hallway to the roof. From that viewpoint, atop one of the tallest buildings in the city, Anthony watched his condo in Abasand burn to the ground, and the block he grew up on, in Beacon Hill, turn to black. Hoffman, who had wanted to be a firefighter since he was in preschool, made one call to his dad but didn't shed a tear. His job was to keep more people from going through the same pain, and that remained his focus.

Meanwhile, on the ground, nurses pushed seventy-three acute-care patients, twenty-three continuing-care patients and a handful of newborns from the neonatal intensive care unit, not to mention the birds and cats from the therapy unit. They were ushered onto city buses and ambulances as smoke seeped into the building and damaged medical equipment, contaminated ventilation and water systems and permanently stained the tile ceilings. The patients evacuated north to an industrial airport, where they were flown on corporate planes to Edmonton's hospitals—yet they were just a tiny fraction of the whole community. Another seventeen thousand people fled to refinery and mining camps up north, but the lion's share had moved south. *Where will they sleep tonight?* I wondered.

Melanie kept me abreast via text of her escape, ending just about every update with *Are you safe?* Rubbing my naked ring finger with regret, I said yes. Was I being honest? I've got fifteen years of experience, but I'd never had to take a stand like this. What I did rely on, though, was my sense of situational awareness—always have the fire in front of you, never behind you, and never park your pumper unless you know your way out. As long as I remembered that, I was telling Melanie the truth. Besides, the more important thing was that they were safe in the camper by Boyle.

As for Mom and Danielle, telling them to go north had been the right call, but it was hard for them to agree later that night when Fort McKay ran out of food and gas. The fire was moving north, and, though it was fifty kilometres away, they felt trapped and decided to return south—back through Fort McMurray, driving on the northbound lane of Highway 63 because the southbound lane was too close to the flames. Mom called to tell me they got through the other end of town, but now they had to get to Edmonton on three-quarters of a tank of gas. I gave them all I could offer: a wish of good luck.

Once word travelled of our roving crew, I got personal cellphone calls from other officers needing extra manpower.

Assistant Deputy Chief Jody Butz called me to check on Silver Springs, just north of the Athabasca River. He didn't have to say much else. I'd done contracting work for him and knew his exact address. We circled the block and deemed it safe. "Silver Springs is all good," I told the boss.

"Thanks," he said. "Now I need you to go to Cartier. Meet with Woykin, find out what's on the go."

We drove the entire perimeter of Thickwood Boulevard/ Confederation Way to find Battalion Chief Mike Woykin's crew, only for him to say the wind had changed directions away from Cartier. "It's not too bad here. Why don't you get back to Wood Buffalo and give Golosky a hand?" he asked.

The sun was long gone now, and the night was not just dark, but pitch-black from the thickness of the smoke. It hovered on the pavement, disguising street signs and making the cookie-cutter residential roads impossible to tell apart. The only light was the dim aura of houses burning behind the billowing smoke. "Golosky's got to be in here somewhere," I said, leaning forwards, chin centimetres from the dash.

The sun was long gone now, and the night was not just dark, but pitch-black from the thickness of the smoke.

We found the battalion chief by spotting the rotating lights on top of his truck. Golosky had a map of the city stretched over the grill.

"We're here to help. Where do you want me?" I asked.

He pointed to a corner of the neighbourhood under threat, but by the time we arrived, there was a fire truck on scene doing all that was needed. We drove back to Golosky and asked for another spot, but sure enough, that hydrant was also occupied. There were firefighters everywhere now, connected to every hydrant. After three attempts and no luck, Golosky said, "I got a call about houses going up in Dickinsfield. Could be rumours, but why don't you check them out?"

So we did—and rumours they were.

Just then Woykin radioed the department. The wind had changed direction, and the fire was pushing into Timberlea again, this time through McKinlay Trailer Park on the northwest tip. "We need men and monitors set up," he said. "It's coming our way."

I felt like a cat chasing a laser pointer, and it was getting to my crew. They grumbled about it almost as loudly as their stomachs. But until there were no orders, there were no breaks. As Hitchcock circled back, I thought I spotted a glow out west, a tiny flash of light far beyond the houses along Tower Road, deep into the forest and sloughs. But nothing had been reported there, and more importantly, *something* had been reported at the McKinlay trailers. So we moved on to our deployment.

"What's happening?" I asked Woykin from the passenger-side window.

"We're getting ready for it—it's coming," he said. "Find yourself a corner and get staged." But it was the same story: every corner and hydrant was occupied.

I walked back to Woykin as he aimed a monitor towards the trees. "Listen," I said, "you're three blocks deep with fire trucks. Not saying I don't want to help, but I can't find room to stage. I saw something by Tower Road. We'll check on that."

"Good idea," he said.

To say there's only one way in and out of Fort McMurray isn't technically true. When the weather is right—meaning terribly cold— Tower Road becomes an "ice road," a concept only people north of sixty degrees latitude understand. Past a short distance of gravel, the frozen sloughs offer a five-hundred-kilometre pathway west. It's important for another reason: it is where the boreal forest and Birchwood Trails connect.

Birchwood Trails is a four-hundred-hectare parkland at the centre of Timberlea's and Thickwood's subdivisions, which form a ring around it. These communities connect through the park's 130 kilometres of recreational trails. We had to keep the fire from getting through any of those subdivisions and into the park, where it could crown in the spruce trees and spread from canopy to canopy, storming into all nine subdivisions. For years, we had felt that Birchwood Trails was a disaster waiting to happen. Lose it, and it's game over.

Hitchcock turned right onto the desolate Tower Road and Cree Road intersection and pulled over next to the ditch along the northwestern community, which backs onto it with one continuous white fence. The distant glow had grown in the bushes along the dirt road. It was redder now, showing that this limb of the fire was heating up and would accelerate towards us. I unscrewed a guardrail so nobody tripped as the crew stretched hoses across the bush. "Set it up again," I said. By now, the strategy required little

> The fire approached like a glowing Goliath, making its war cry with blowing embers.

explaining. They covered more ground with wyes, adapter splits allowing for two guys per line, running in opposite directions at my orders.

It was an ominous feeling, waiting for battle. My crew stood armed, at the ready, like knights in a dragon fight, but with nozzles as swords and little armour to speak of. The fire approached like a glowing Goliath, making its war cry with blowing embers. Recognizing the potential disaster, I called for support. Saprae Creek and Fort McKay volunteers arrived.

"What do you need?" asked a volunteer captain.

"Hot spots," I said. "I need piss packs, hoses, shovels, jump fences, get 'em out." By now it was a well-oiled machine. The orders were simple.

"Over there," I yelled. "Shed on fire."

They sprinted after it, along with Hitchcock, who jumped off the truck with a chainsaw to tear through the fence. The volunteers blasted the wooden shed, exposing a pile of paint cans and a mini-fridge.

"What do we have here?" wondered Hitchcock, entering the smouldering shed they had just extinguished. He popped open the door and his face lit up. A fruit basket, a loaf of bread, cans of juice.

He emerged from the fence opening with a garbage bag full of goodies slung over his shoulder. "Hey, Cap, you want a drink?" he asked with his mouth full, and handed me a can of Minute Maid. "How about a banana?" My first snack since noon, it was the best damn banana and orange juice I'd ever had. My drooling alone could have extinguished the wildfire.

I helped Kyle distribute the bounty to the others. Pellegrin quickly crammed a slice of bread into her mouth with a filthy hand before the nozzle reaction broke from her grip. She wiped the dripping water off her face and fastened her grip on the ice-cold hose.

Sitting at the end of that hose was like riding through Niagara Falls on the *Maid of the Mist*—even for me, standing ten feet behind. If this were winter, their boots would be frozen to the road, but instead we were creating a mud swamp, and every boot was a water vessel. The probies' once spotless yellow coveralls were dyed grey. Gusts of wind shoved potent plumes into our faces. We should have all had T-1000 canister-style full respirator masks—what forestry firefighters carry instead of air tanks—but our department's supply disappeared quickly, and the air tanks on our truck had long been emptied. So, at best, some of us had safety glasses and paper medical masks. Despite all those inadequacies, we remained, all hands on deck. The bushes were soaked thirty feet deep, but we'd have to wait for the fire to come to our line to know if our defence worked.

The crackling of trees grew louder, and while the sweat on my neck dripped into my uniform, my uniform itself was drying out.

"Don't drop your nozzles until I say so," I ordered. "It's about to get hot."

The flames leaped forwards from the canopies, dancing thirty feet above us, but as they hit the water wall the energy was sucked right out of the forest. "Hit the canopies. Up and down, just like that. More surface area at ninety degrees. Nice work, Heikel, you're hitting your stride. Kill those embers." He raised his nozzle, left, right, up, down, spraying everything that looked hot.

The fire was cowering, shrinking before our eyes and struggling to get past our guard with laboured puffs of smoke. "Good, good, lower your nozzles—hit it in the centre. Extend your lines and move in farther."

We battled it for hours, half the men on primary fire, the other half on hot spots, switching on and off whenever arms started weakening or a bathroom break was needed. As the flames dwindled, I could exhale, knowing we had dulled it to a small roar. I handed the site off to the volunteers, since it was just cooling and searching for hot spots from here. An entire neighbourhood saved by a couple of trucks with small crews. McKinlay was another story.

Captain Hamm and his crew were under heavy attack and calling for support in the trailer court when we returned. Most of these mobile homes were combusting in record time due to their small sizes and highly synthetic exteriors. The smoke was intensely black and toxic—guys were struggling to keep up with the pace, and everyone was more than a little concerned about lung damage.

Of the hundred trailers along McKinlay Crescent, about twenty of them caught fire, and most were lost causes, but it was largely under control. Still, there was a lot of work to be done and I was determined to stay, even if there weren't enough hose lines for everyone. My crew sprayed what they could, hit the hot spots, cleaned up along the edges and racked hoses while two crash trucks sprayed heavy-duty foam everywhere.

They don't see many house fires, these industry guys, so they relied on me for direction. "That looks like it could spread," I said to a crash operator, pointing at a trailer. It cruised onto the lawn, extended its turbo-charged nozzle on a long crane and revved up. With a warbly scream, it blasted two thousand litres in one minute—three times the volume of a city pump—until the tank was empty. When the water cleared, the flames were extinguished, as were the windows, eaves and decorative lamps.

The roving machine backed up to fetch more water from a hydrant, two guys from Jeff Hamm's crew stepped in with hand lines to cool it, and I walked between the trailers to make sure the flames didn't spread. They had, melting the vinyl siding and starting to light the roof. Just as I turned back, I heard turbo revving. I looked up to see the crash's nozzle pointed right at me. "Oh crap!" I yelped, jumping behind the trailer like a rabbit in the bush just in time to dodge a stream that surely would have bruised a rib or two or twenty.

Meanwhile, some of the probies were struggling with defensive attacks—the concept of spraying the thing you don't want to catch fire—sometimes taking the strategy too far. Relph approached Sabey, who was angrily sitting on a hose line, drenched like he'd just gotten out of a swimming pool in his coveralls. "What the hell happened to you?" asked Relph.

"A volunteer thought it'd be a good idea to soak me in case I caught fire," he complained. "Soaked my ass with a full fire hose."

Relph laughed. "I'll make sure I move four feet to the right. Ready to switch out?"

"Gladly," said Sabey, wringing half a cup of water out of his hair after he passed the hose.

Relph moved the line a safe distance from the culprit, but too deep into the smoke. A firefighter on the other side of the house didn't spot him and drenched him from head to toe. "Goddamn it!" shouted Relph, a hard guy to provoke—even after possibly losing his house in Abasand.

"Sorry," said the faint voice behind the smoke.

Relph had been there for four beleaguering hours. His vehicle was one of the first there, before any pumps arrived, when only four trailers had been fully involved. He spotted Jamieson and Shantz in their duty uniforms, busting fences with chainsaws to pull lines up a street through backyards. It wasn't hero work, but it was a necessary grind. "Hey," Relph called to a spectating probie. "Take this a minute, would you, please?"

Relph, dripping all over, rose to his feet, passed the nozzle, headed over to his friends and fell into step with them. "More hands, less effort," he said as the two welcomed him.

It was early morning, and, though I didn't feel at all tired, I could have sworn I was hallucinating civilians loading stuff into the back of a pickup. "What is that?" muttered Kyle, standing with me by Pumper 310. He and another firefighter went to check it out.

They trudged towards the two guys, getting ankle deep in a minor flood caused by the sewers overflowing from extreme hose runoff.

"Guys, what are you still doing here?" Hitchcock asked.

"We're just loading our tools," said one indignantly.

"Tools? You can replace tools. Get out of here."

"Just help us out."

Hitchcock could tell by the looks on their faces that it would be easier to help the two guys out than it would be to argue with them.

"Let's just get them out of here," he said.

"Fine," the new guy scoffed.

It was easier said than done. The guys had hockey bags full of metal industrial tools, each weighing hundreds of pounds.

Nonstop firefighting was exhausting Hitchcock, but he kept his professionalism while the new guy complained. "Why are we still here? You can't save these trailers."

"Captain's still in the fight, so we're still in the fight," said Hitchcock.

I overheard it from the sideline and was proud of the way he dealt with it. But a couple of hours later, as the sun rose and the trailers were steaming piles, I noticed the group losing their grip. We had been going nonstop for nineteen hours. They were sitting on deck chairs, disgruntled, stretching sore muscles and complaining that they were tired, needed sleep, weren't sure why the hell we were still here, didn't understand the point anymore.

I approached Hitchcock and nodded my head for him to follow me out of earshot. We walked a few paces into the street. "I know you're worn out, but I wanted to let you know I'm proud of the way you've stepped up. You all have—I know it's been tough, but you're doing a great job."

"Thanks," he said, a little surprised. "I know how important it is to have everyone on board."

"Did you call your mom?" I asked. "You tell her you're all right?" He nodded. "Call her again just in case." I looked at my watch—5:30 a.m.—and looked back to the fire. There was so much to do. Those old Smokey the Bear PSAs came back to me. "Drown the fire, stir it, drown it, stir it." If we left now, it would be like pouring a cup of water on a campfire and walking away. But the park was surrounded by dirt, and until the heat rose there was no risk of the flames jumping into adjoining houses. With so many bodies on the site, we could afford to leave.

"We'll go to hall 5 for some rest," I told Hitchcock.

The cool of dawn air compressed smoke to the ground like mist in a horror movie, and we drove to the hall in a dreamlike environment. Hundreds of house lights illuminated empty rooms, and in some of their front yards, deer chomped on the grass and flower-beds, unfazed by the violent nature around them. I overheard Heikel on the phone with his wife: "We did good. I think this is the worst of it. If you're still north of town, you should head south now. I think 63 is clear." He was right about one thing: the highway was open.

Before I got out of the truck, Heikel came to the passenger side and said, "Thank you for your leadership—thank you for keeping us safe."

I shook his hand and said, "I want everyone up and on the truck by nine."

The firefighters collapsed in the TV room recliners, their necks chapped from wearing N95 bands all day, and the bridges of their noses looking like they could have been scarred for life by the masks. "If you wake up before me," Matthew said to Christine beside him, "wake me up. I don't want to be useless. I wanna do shit."

"Ditto," she said.

Hitchcock wanted to be alone and, just as well, clean. All the beds were taken besides the captain's dorm room. "Go ahead," I said. "I won't be sleeping anyways." He entered the captains' office quarters, kicked off his soaked boots, had a shower and borrowed my stick of deodorant, towels and Q-Tips. Then he rolled onto the captains' bed and was asleep before his head hit the pillow.

CHAPTER 7

RECONNAISSANCE

I t was a strange feeling to know the world was watching us. Every news outlet around the world, from CNN to the BBC to the *Times of India*, had turned to Northern Canada for what was clearly a historic moment, an event that would be studied and written about with grandiosity comparable to the Great Chicago Fire. Would historians see it as a case study in successful urban and wild land interface firefighting, or a cautionary tale?

It was too early to know for sure if anybody had perished, since so many McMurrayites do shift work, arriving home in the early morning and slumbering through the late afternoon. Every door was banged on, but not every one was opened, so there was no way to know if anyone had slept through it, or woke up before it was too late. So far, at least, we knew for sure that no firefighters had suffered injuries beyond a sprained ankle and smoke exhaustion. That was a success in itself.

Not long before, in June 2013, nineteen of twenty firefighters died in a wild land blaze near Yarnell, Arizona. The workplace safety commission of Arizona said a dangerous order from above had wrongly prioritized some properties over their safety, sending them into harm's way just before the winds whipped the inferno into an inescapable firestorm. And then there was the infamous Mann Gulch Fire of 1949—aerial firefighting's early years—that killed thirteen smoke jumpers between the ages of nineteen and twenty-eight. They parachuted into the scene just minutes before a "cross-over," which is when a fire line reaches such intensity it morphs into violent convection.

Tuesday's dry air mass, combined with hot temperatures and winds ranging from forty to seventy kilometres, meant we had certainly fought in crossover conditions. The fire swallowed so much fuel, releasing so much energy that it created its own weather. In the most intense areas, you could spot a species of smoke columns more common in volcanic eruptions, called pyro cumulus clouds. These fire clouds punched into Wood Buffalo's upper atmosphere, creating dry lightning that propagated the fire in three spots, spreading the Beast's tentacles even farther. That was out in the woodlands, so I didn't see it with my own eyes, but Forestry guys we'd worked with buzzed about rain-less and thunder-less lightning storms, as if they were standing inside a plasma globe.

> The fire swallowed so much fuel, releasing so much energy that it created its own weather.

That, so far, we were all healthy enough to fight another day was owed to the safety culture of Canadian fire-fighting. We try to avoid putting ourselves in front of the flames, especially when dealing with crown fires, whose flames can sprout two or three times the tree height, consuming whole canopies of bush at wicked paces. At best, we use indirect tactics to battle them—dropping tanker retardants and using firebreaks to corral the fire—or heli-torch or back-burn the bush, essentially fighting fire with fire by burning controlled areas to deplete ground fuel. But, for the most part, we fight fires from the back side—where the fire's already destroyed—because that's the safest place to be, and we squeeze it to a point or try to redirect it with firebreaks. A good rule of thumb is to have one foot in the green and one in the black. That way, if a fire turns around, as this one had several times thanks to the erratic winds, then it torches an area where there's no fuel left, providing a perfect escape route and safety zone. But you can only determine that when the sun is up; that's why we never fight wildfires at night—you can't track the smoke columns to determine the location of the fuel loads or the wind direction. You can't predict the fire's behaviour. Only structural fires can be fought in the dark, so MWF-009 was a different character altogether, testing our wild land and urban firefighting skills at once.

As the sun floated higher in the hazy sky and the temperatures climbed to an unseasonably high degree, we knew it would be a long haul. Ten thousand hectares of the boreal zone were blazing, and the air quality index of sixteen was almost double what's considered a very high health risk. The night before, while we were busy on Tower Road in Thickwood, REOC had said as much in a press briefing. "The worst of the fire is not over," warned Alberta Forestry's Bernie Schmitte. "We're still faced with high temperatures, low humidity and strong winds." The fire chief said we were going to be there for "quite a period of time," without any indication of how long. I should have been gathering my strength, but I was uninterested in rest before the next battle.

The next morning, after arriving at Fire Hall 5, I took the elevator up to the second floor to see if I could get an update from ADC Butz. He'd just arrived from an aerial reconnaissance and had a good visual of the damage. Butz had been prepared for the worst after a night of mayhem, when all he'd heard through the radio was an endless string of reports of entire communities on fire. Everyone expected the worst, especially for Abasand, Waterways and Beacon Hill. Seen from up in the chopper, the devastation was unreal. About fifteen hundred structures had been destroyed between them. Wood Buffalo lost forty homes, and in Timberlea, where we fought until sunrise, thirteen trailers were obliterated. Spot fires destroyed four houses in Grayling Terrace (north of Abasand), one in Thickwood (east of Wood Buffalo) and two downtown. But given the rumours of neighbourhoods wiped off the map, Jody was relieved to see that wasn't the case. Returning to REOC with news that 70 percent of Beacon Hill was lost actually gave people hope about the 30 percent that was saved. He sent a fleet of water bombers to "red tarp" Beacon Hill and keep it that way.

In a sense, we were winning the fight, but it didn't calm down the REOC. There was no way I was getting a word in with Butz in the flurry of action; even Michaela Melosky, that twenty-two-year-old student from Victoria, was overwhelmed. She'd spent the night before picking up stragglers around downtown—anyone who didn't have transportation, like homeless, single moms or new immigrants—and bringing them to Mac Island for safety. Her boss, Fort McMurray's deputy director of emergency management, tried to get her to leave with civilians on a transit bus to Edmonton. Taken in by the spirit of a foreign community coming together to save their city, Michaela refused. "If I'm useful to you," she told him, "then I'm staying."

I spent the rest of the morning kicking around the hall, talking to other officers and having a brief chat with mechanics about Pumper 310. We must've taken five years off it that day, but the old gal would have to hold up.

I called Mom to let her know I was safe but wouldn't be able to communicate much further. The family had just arrived in Redwater, a town outside Edmonton that took them nine hours to reach instead of the usual three and a half. Danielle had pulled over for some shut-eye, as did her husband, Brian, in the car behind them. In a few hours, they'd arrive at a family friend's in Edmonton for shelter.

Every Albertan who had a friend or relative in Fort McMurray threw open their doors, pulled out a futon, spared a bedroom for them, while other McMurrayites relied on the charity of community groups scrambling to turn churches, halls and temples into refugee camps. They scrounged whatever they could: cots, sleeping bags, air mattresses. One Edmonton mosque stacked prayer carpets into makeshift beds for anyone of any faith. In Calgary, a group of Syrian refugees who'd escaped a literal war zone just months before grouped together to donate clothes, furniture, hygiene products and toys to evacuees, or to just cook breakfast for the arrivals. By Wednesday morning, the Edmonton Public School Board would welcome any Wood Buffalo student whose parents didn't want them to miss a day of class. West Edmonton Mall gave McMurrayites free passes to its theme park and collected diapers, pillows, socks and underwear from shoppers on a life-sized replica of Christopher Columbus's *Santa María* ship. The city's expo centre, Northlands, had welcomed five hundred people by Wednesday afternoon and was prepared for five thousand more. Up north, the usually competitive industry camps that infamously house the "shadow population" banded together to house twenty-five thousand people. And in the town of Lac La Biche, the population quadrupled as the town's hotels, houses and campgrounds absorbed some twelve thousand of my neighbours. Some Albertans didn't wait for our community to come to their doors; they brought diapers, fuel and food up to the evacuees stranded on the highways. All across the nation, and around the world, the motto was "Fort Mac Strong," as relief funds surpassed a million dollars in a day.

> All across the nation, and around the world, the motto was "Fort Mac Strong," as relief funds surpassed a million dollars in a day.

The business community stepped up too, whether it was Alberta-wide restaurants offering free sandwiches and drinks, a Lac La Biche barber advertising free hot shaves or WestJet Airlines sending planes to industrial airports to rescue civilians who were trapped after the fire choked off the highway.

That was the beauty in the Beast, but things weren't as glamorous at hall 5. Just a decent meal would suffice. But the RCMP's supply dump from the grocery stores that had generously allowed them to raid their shelves amounted to some bags of fruit, a few boxes of granola bars and pallets of water bottles. All of which I was happy to replenish with, but we were hankering for hot food.

Training Officer Martin Kratochvil was gathering supplies when I entered the kitchen. "How you holding up, Asher?" he asked.

My hair was disheveled and I was still in my stinking, muddy uniform. A day and a half's worth of fumes kept me coughing like a bad cold. "Great," I said. "Ready to get on the pump."

"You're a champ, man," he said. "You get eh-fracks?"

I had no idea what he was talking about.

"Alberta First Responder Radio Communications System."

"Uh. Huh."

"AFRCCS," he repeated. "Guy from the government turned up with a trailer full of these two-way radios that RCMP use. They work on a specific government network. Since the radio tower burned up last night—"

"—the radio—"

"Yeah, it's done. So you'll need one of these for dispatch. They're giving them out at Mac Island. Incident Command moved there from hall 1. It's staging now."

Staging is a central place to gather equipment and disperse it where it's needed, especially when the needs outweigh the resources. Any time there's a catastrophe or mass casualty event, say a four-car pileup, we'll set up a treatment sector, transport sector and a staging sector, so that we can manage the event efficiently and consistently. With fire trucks from all over Alberta arriving, we needed a bigger area to organize what would soon be close to a thousand firefighters, up from 152 when I started.

"Here," said Marty, handing me the handheld radio from his waist. "You're headed back out. I'll get myself another."

I strode into the TV lounge to peel the sleeping crew off the leather recliners. They were slow to get up, but the mention of food got them going. I didn't stick around to see their looks of disappointment when they realized "food" was basically something they could have purchased from a vending machine. Instead, I went into the captains' dorm to shake Hitchcock awake. "Come on," I said, nudging his shoulder. "Everyone's tired, but there's work to be done."

"Thanks, Cap," he said.

"Quick truck check, then back to the job," I replied.

Pumper 310 was in disarray, but Hitchcock, Heikel and Pellegrin swept it out quickly, organized the hoses and nozzles and accounted for all the shovels, piss-packs and our lone ground monitor. Incredibly, it was all there. Even the pencils in the glove compartment.

Though I had my radio, I didn't know how to use it and needed to stop at Mac Island for a tutorial. I was also desperate to know what was going on with staging. When there's a catastrophe on this scale, it's not enough simply to have a central place to distribute and organize apparatus, but you need to replenish basic things—masks and fresh socks, for example—plus serve proper meals to fuel your personnel.

It was late morning and the inversion hadn't lifted yet, so time allowed it. There was even a moment to spray water into the flaming foundations of the two houses that perished in Grayling Terrace nearby Mac Island. Some of the crew wanted to roll by their own houses, make sure they were still standing, and Hitchcock continued to earn that totally imaginary World's Best Ex-boyfriend honour with a stopover at his ex's house to turn on her sprinkler and text her photographic evidence that it was still standing. My own home was in the clear. The fire, so far, had stayed on the west side of the city, and, technically speaking, Saprae Creek, the furthest eastern community, wasn't under mandatory evacuation yet. I texted Melanie to let her know.

Saprae is looking good

Are they letting anybody into
Fort McMurray?

It could be a while
Buy the kids fresh clothes if you need

We arrived at Mac Island in the late morning, but already the weather was creeping up to 32 Celsius again. Our skin was as red as the sky, and I was sweating even before the first battle of the day— which was sure to come around noon again.

Just off Franklin Avenue, sitting on a 240-acre islet where the Athabasca and Clearwater rivers fork, Mac Island is so big that inside, street signs point you around to either of the two NHL-sized rinks or two field houses, towards eight curling sheets, to an indoor running track or squash courts, to ballrooms and, for when the freeze scares even children away, to an indoor playground. When it opened in 2009, the sleek building—a curvy glass and steel body and a wave-like awning over a massive amphitheatre stage—was a show of the new oil capital's prowess. But with the economy floundering, it'd become one of the more affordable ways to spend an afternoon with the family. Still, I'd never seen it like this before.

The semicircular parking lot was stuffed with fleet vehicles, fire engines, tow trucks, dozers, news vans and double-parked, abandoned civilian cars, and was spray-painted heavily to label stocks of equipment. Men in uniform confabbed outside the reflective glass exterior. Inside was abuzz with activity—firefighters I'd never seen before slipping into bunker gear, or ones I recognized pulling unused cots out of boxes and assembling them for places to rest. People barked orders across halls; others talked loudly into their phones trying to be heard over the racket. It was hard to tell who was working for whom.

A woman pushed a dolly of water bottle pallets, and our crew followed, past artificial palm trees in the tropical-themed water park, and past the public library, where everyone from RCMP officers to transient McMurrayites catnapped on cots or the carpeted floor. The woman led us to a gymnasium where they'd delivered the food.

I couldn't believe what I was looking at: a hundred shopping carts' worth of random stuff, the results of the authorized grocery store raids, had been unloaded on the floor. Just heaps of cereal boxes, milk, bread, soup cans, Kraft dinner and Hamburger Helper—and not a damn thing to cook it with or eat it out of. It was mixed together with toilet paper, bathroom wipes, toothbrushes and ChapSticks.

"No," I said, shaking my head in disbelief. "No. What is this? This is a joke." I turned to the crew. "Is this real? Am I seeing this?"

Heikel just shrugged, while the rest stuffed their pockets with energy bars. I called REOC. "Whoever's in charge of food at Mac Island, put them on," I demanded.

It was Michael Powlesland, the city's procurement supervisor, now in charge of logistics.

"Something needs to be done with this food. You need to get

a crew in here and you need to start managing this place," I said sternly.

"I don't understand," he replied. "We gave you food. What more do you want?"

"I want a hot meal."

"Where am I supposed to get you a hot meal from?" he snapped back. "Every cook in town is gone. We asked the restaurants to keep their kitchens open for you, but we couldn't force them. This is the best we could do."

My focus narrowed on a football-sized, plastic-wrapped hunk of ham in the pile. "This is the best you could do?" I asked. "There's a fucking ham. On the floor. Of Mac Island. A ham!"

"Look, you've got what you've got. If you don't want to eat it, don't eat it."

Fatigue, frustration and hunger washed over me. "I don't want a cold ham—a fucking floor ham. I want someone here, right now, cooking me a ham supper!" I could hear my crew and bystanders snickering, but I was dead serious.

"If your guys put it in the fridge it wouldn't be a floor ham—" said Michael.

"We're firefighters. Not site coordinators."

"You're just being unrealistic now."

"I'm being unrealistic?" I took a deep, calming breath. "No, you've got raw meat, eggs, just sitting here. Raw food, unprepared, with no means to prepare it. That sounds pretty unrealistic, doesn't it? Get someone here to look after it." I hung up and stuffed my phone into my pants pocket, huffing with anger.

I didn't know it at the time, but just hours prior, Michael Powlesland had been escorted to his townhouse in Beacon Hill, where he discovered that he'd lost everything, including his chihuahua, Whiskey. It was a reminder to never lose my cool.

After loading water and bars into my pockets, and applying ChapStick—much needed after the smoke had dried out my mucus membranes and left my lips dry as bone—I got a quick briefing on how to use the radios from someone representing Canada Task Force 2.

Can-TF2, as it's known, is a rapid-deployment-response team that swoops in to assist local authorities in the wake of large-scale hazards and disasters. Mostly from the Calgary area, Can-TF2 assists anywhere in the world, but the dozens of team members—from search and rescue, medical, emergency management and water purification—didn't have to travel far for this deployment. The team helped my colleague Captain Steve Hansen direct staging after Incident Command was moved here from hall 1. His role, essentially, was helping the department track its resources and build a game plan. At the moment, the strategy was to simply reestablish the level of command after a day of havoc. Every battalion chief was given a quadrant of the larger Wood Buffalo region, and Hansen was directing us to each one depending on whether they needed another truck or a water tanker. I was glad not to be stuck in staging—I wanted to be out on the pump, in the line of fire. ADC Butz wanted me there too, and personally called me again for another deployment.

The fire had leaped the Clearwater River through Waterways on Tuesday; now it had leaped back over the river, pushing southwest towards town. The neighbourhood of Gregoire, across from the now razed Super 8 motel and gas station on Highway 63, was in its scope. Hansen and Jody sent twenty trucks there.

It was noon. The smoke, once a thick plume hovering about us, had snapped loose with rising temperatures and was blowing angrily over the highway. Gregoire is twenty kilometres from Saprae, and should the wind shift east again, there was nothing but volatile fuel connecting the two communities. My phone pinged. It was Melanie.

Rumour is that saprae is in
danger now.

Yea it just jumped the ravine.
We are sending 20 trucks to try
and hold it

Fuckkk

Fire Hall 2—the depart-
ment's dispatch and
communications centre
on ordinary days—
needed protection in
Gregoire. We couldn't
afford to lose it.

I flicked my ringer setting to vibrate. No more distractions. Fire Hall 2—the department's dispatch and communications centre on ordinary days—needed protection in Gregoire. We couldn't afford to lose it.

Hitchcock parked Pumper 310 next to the small brown building in between a trailer court and an RV lot. The firefighters connected hose to hydrant, snaking hand lines around two communications towers surrounded by chain-link fences. Hitchcock popped the steamer port and turned to me stunned. "Uhh, Cap," he said. "There's no water."

"Go one up, one back," I said, pointing to hydrants on opposite sides of Gregoire Drive. "Try them all down the line."

"Cap," he said firmly. "There's *no water*. The system's drained."

The Ashers in 1980 (*clockwise from top left*): Peggy, Bill, Damian (age three) and Danielle.

PEGGY ASHER

Damian Asher, seventeen, as warrant officer first-class, leading the year-end parade of 868 Royal Canadian Air Cadets, Fort McMurray.

PEGGY ASHER

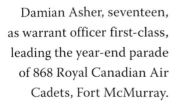

Aerial view of Fort McMurray, looking south into downtown.

WOOD BUFFALO ENVIRONMENTAL ASSOCIATION/CURTIS COMEAU

Looking west from Fire Hall 5's hose tower on Monday, May 2, 2016—the evening before the evacuation.

MATTHEW HEIKEL

The gridlock on Highway 63 outside Fort McMurray.

Franklin Avenue in downtown Fort McMurray after the evacuation.

The Abasand staging area on May 4, 2016, as the fire blazed in Horse River Valley.

The Chateau Nova inferno on the evening of May 4, 2016.

MATTHEW HEIKEL

Fire at the northern end of Siltstone Place in Stonecreek (before the bulldozing).

MATTHEW HEIKEL

Derrick Appeit and Kyle Hitchcock (*front*) on an attack line, soaking fiery piles of debris after bulldozing houses in Timberlea on the morning of May 5, 2016.

EDWARD GRAINGER

A crescent in Grayling Terrace in ruins.

Jordan Hanthorn preemptively soaking houses in Ermine on May 3, 2016.

The abandoned Highway 63, looking north to the city.

A chopper delivers a "Bambi Bucket" in Walnut Crescent.

MIKE WOYKIN

Cooling a lost home in Walnut Crescent.

MIKE WOYKIN

A bulldozer lost and abandoned on Stonecreek Landing after the May 4 and 5 blaze.

MATTHEW HEIKEL

Christine Pellegrin observing the devastation in Wood Buffalo after the epic battle.

MATTHEW HEIKEL

The remains of a partially melted swing set in a residential neighbourhood.

SCOTT OLSON/GETTY IMAGES

Donated shoes are offered to evacuees at an evacuation center on May 7, 2016, in Lac La Biche, Alberta.

SCOTT OLSON/GETTY IMAGES

On his first free night, May 9, 2016, Damian Asher makes a surprise visit to the family camper in Boyle. He's embraced by his son, Aidan, and daughter, Taya.

MELANIE ASHER

Firefighters welcome McMurrayites home in early June 2016.

BLOOMBERG/GETTY IMAGES

As residents return to Fort McMurray, a restoration worker cleans a downtown shop on June 3, 2016.

COLE BURSTON/GETTY IMAGES

Monday, May 9, 2016: One of FMFD's first rotation shifts since the evacuation (*clockwise from top left*): Cpt. Damian Asher, Trevor Shantz, Joe Jamieson, Kyle Hitchcock, Chris Relph.

Damian Asher rebuilding his home in Saprae Creek, alone, in the dead of winter.

OMAR MOUALLEM

CHAPTER 8

CRITICAL INFRASTRUCTURE

When a wildfire crosses boundaries into human habitat, there are three priorities for firefighters. Number one is protecting human life, civilian and firefighter. After that, it's protecting homes. The third priority is protecting critical infrastructure, and there's no infrastructure more critical than the water treatment plant. Without it, you undermine the first two priorities.

Fort McMurray's Water Treatment Centre, a long rectangular building perched on the edge of the Athabasca River between Mac Island and Thickwood, was having an epic battle. First the fire roared north towards the plant through Abasand on Tuesday afternoon, then from the west when it busted through Wood Buffalo. Twelve staffers led by Guy Jette, the plant manager for over three decades, stayed in the control room for as long as they could, even as smoke seeped into the buildings and interfered with the reservoir gauges, turning the charts of water pressure and flow on their computer screens into foreboding question marks. While Jette struggled with lost communications, he also squabbled with his wife, who had brought their kids to the plant, refusing to leave the city without him. He had a hell of a time convincing her that he'd be okay, that he had sufficient escape routes. Truth is, one of those escape routes was the river itself.

Jette and his team were also prepared to violate a basic public health measure and pump dirty river water into the plant reservoir because water supply was scarce. With nearly every hydrant activated, tens of thousands of sprinklers in use, and an unknowable number of waterlines leaking in damaged houses, the centre was pushing three times as much fluid as normal—nearly ninety million litres a day. The city had installed four new filters that could double the output, but the equipment required a twenty-four-hour bacteria test before going online. They prepared for this—the best-case scenario—but Jette also had Syncrude connect a big pump from the river to the reservoir. All it would take was two connections and one key turn to contaminate every water pipe, forcing a boil water advisory that could last for months.

On Wednesday afternoon, with limited water supply and critical equipment wrecked, the water treatment team had no means of knowing the neediest areas. Best they could do was peer out the control room window, try to infer where the flames were largest or nearest to houses and direct the water supply there. The fire approaching Gregoire was way on the southern tip, well out of view from the water treatment plant, so we'd need to get crafty if we wanted to protect hall 2.

I requested a portable pond. Saprae Creek's volunteer crew arrived at the hall twenty minutes later with a small water truck and one ten-thousand-litre pumpkin. We drained the red tanker's supply into the pumpkin, and we soaked the brown building with every drop. This was a trial run. We knew it wasn't going to be enough.

"What are we going to do?" asked Hitchcock.

"I'm going to get more tankers," I replied, radioing for three forty-thousand-litre tankers.

"I don't think it's going to be enough."

"Probably not," I admitted. "But it'll be enough to keep it off the building." I gathered the crew and laid out the plan: "We'll wait till the fire's on top of us, fight with everything we have, then pack up and run. We won't be able to worry about the RV lot or anything else but the hall. It's going to be dicey. Plan your exit strategy for your hose line on your own, keep track of your partner, work in trios."

The dispatch girls evacuated the hall before we finished setting up. Somewhere behind the brown plumes, the sun peaked on the horizon, showering us in radiant heat. Heikel and Hitchcock stripped down to their T-shirts and uniform pants. When I entered the building, hoping to pillage its water bottles, I was blasted with a glorious breeze. "Holy crap, guys," I called, head sticking out the front doors. "There's air-conditioning in here. We have time before the tanker arrives. Take a rest." The crew dragged chairs, or splayed on the floor, kicking off their boots and basking under the vents for a short coffee break. Finding adequate caffeine had become a constant struggle.

> Somewhere behind the brown plumes, the sun peaked on the horizon, showering us in radiant heat.

I stayed outside and stood watch. The flames were about a kilometre away, blowing west from the other side of a creek, but it looked to me like they were dulling down. I hoped my eyes weren't deceiving me. Sipping coffee, I opened the Facebook app on my phone and quickly wrote a rare message to my friends, letting them know I was okay, and that we were fully recharged. *Bring it on, we won't stop*, I typed and posted.

As I scrolled through my feed, I saw a stream of terrible news. The fire had claimed its first two casualties in a most insidious way; a few kilometres from refuge in Heart Lake First Nation, two hundred kilometres south, a tractor trailer unit had collided with an SUV during the chaotic evacuation. The accident killed the driver and the passenger—their names not yet known, but they were residents of Saprae Creek.

In the background, I listened to my radio. Crews were still in Abasand doing what they could with no water. They would remove a house from the path of the fire, reducing its fuel and creating a firebreak. I wanted to be there with them, but my orders were clear. No one would be able to do their jobs if we lost hall 2, our 9-1-1 dispatcher. Every job was as important as the next, and this was mine.

Before the tanker arrived, I spotted the crews of Captains Mark Pomeroy and Pat Duggin patrolling Gregoire, monitoring its outer loop for hot spots. The trucks entered the parking lot, and the captains got out. "It's looking good," said Pomeroy.

"We don't think it's going to crest in the houses," Duggin added. "Wind's dying down."

I looked in the back of Pumper 311. Morari and four firefighters guzzled water bottles and took turns squeezing a bottle of Tetracaine into their red eyes to cool the burning.

"You all look like you could cool off a bit," I said. "The boys are inside and the AC is still on." Duggin and Pomeroy are two veteran captains. They knew they couldn't stay long. But they also understood the importance of replenishing morale.

As Morari made her way to the hall, I checked in with her to see if her kids got out of town safely. She and Steve had babysat Taya and Aidan a number of times, and I'd met her boys when I assisted with their home inspection. I hoped Briggs and Maddox weren't still stuck at the hall without a mother or father.

Luckily, when Steve's crew came to rest, after 1:00 a.m., he had gathered the kids from a room with dozens of other firefighters' kids, dogs and a few haggard girlfriends looking after this panicked day-care. The boys were overjoyed to see their dad, and reluctant to let go of him as he placed them in the SUV. They headed to Fort McKay First Nation, where his colleague lived, and Steve hoped to be back in an hour, assuming the sixty-kilometre road was cleared. By the time he reached the edge of the city limits, he wondered if he'd lose the spot on his own truck.

The lanes were jammed as gassed-out cars clogged the highway. While he drove ten kilometres per hour, the kids wailed and begged to go home, scared witless by the apocalyptic scene outside their windows: folks were strewn across the ditches, rolled up in sleeping bags or shivering without, or camping in tents on the side of the road.

They finally arrived at Steve's friend's around five. Briggs was fast asleep, but Maddox had refused to close his eyes and risk letting his dad out of his sight again. Steve stayed by his son's side, reassuring him they'd be okay, that Mommy and Daddy would beat the fire and, although he knew it wasn't a promise he could keep, that their home was going to be there when they got back. He called around Fort McKay and arranged for someone to pick them up the next day and get them to Saskatchewan, then drove back to hall 1, arriving in time to work again without a wink of sleep.

After Captain Pomeroy's truck left, I called to hear the kids' voices for the first time in what felt like weeks: "We're working really hard to save the city," I said. "I don't know when yet, but I promise I'll see you soon."

Three houses and three hours later, the fire was only half a kilometre away from hall 2, cresting the hill into the back end of Gregoire as the wind shifted and the flames started pushing east. ADC Butz called with orders to leave Fire Hall 2. "The fire alarms are ringing at the landfill," he said. "Can you get over there?"

As we crossed the intersection over McKenzie Boulevard and turned onto Highway 63 south, the road was completely black. The literal Dumpster fire blew rancid, thick smoke over the land. We couldn't see two metres in front of us, couldn't tell if there were parked cars in our way or a wall of flames. I leaned against the dashboard, squinting through the heavy smoke, and Hitchcock did his best to follow the road's yellow line. We passed the gates to the landfill and descended into the valley, trying to reach the admin building at the top of the hill on the far side. Our air-conditioning was on full blast, but it was just blowing hot air.

> Idling through the valley, Hitchcock and I peered through the windshield, trying to navigate the thick, black smoke.

"Drive faster," someone yelled. The radiant heat punching through the windows told us we were nearing the blaze, but it was unbearable.

Idling through the valley, Hitchcock and I peered through the windshield, trying to navigate the thick, black smoke. The heat intensified, but finally, the smoke cleared and we got a glimpse of our surroundings. We saw fire tornadoes in the trees on either side of the road. Dressed in a reddish-black aura, they whirled fifty metres into the sky. When we reached the admin office, it was surrounded by spot fires—in the trash, in the parched grass— but the building itself was safe because it was metal-clad. It wasn't going anywhere. I let Jody know.

"Asher," he said with eerie quietness. "It's pushing towards the airport. They just issued evacuation orders for Saprae."

Wed, May 3, 3:50 PM

Wind is pushing hard towards saprae

Ok
Shit
Is it on airport road

Not sure

Are you in gregoire still

Yea I think we have 60 km plus winds

Fuck

I hear they have massive pumps in
saline creek camp holding it

Ok good

Saline Creek is a subdivision under construction between the Prairie Creek neighbourhood and Saprae, eleven kilometres to the west. The Horse River Fire crawled east from the dump and encroached on Fire Hall 5 in the mid-afternoon. REOC was faced with the decision to relocate south to Nexen work camp, and then to Lac La Biche. ADC Butz and three others stayed back and kept communications in order while firefighters outside protected the property.

Just as Butz told me, the fire was moving towards my home, but the Prairie Creek area was under attack and undermanned. Pomeroy and Duggin were among the first there, set up on the western edge of the neighbourhood on Rodeo Drive, trying to keep the fire in the trees. The bush was scorched, and as it dulled down you could see through to the highway and beyond for miles. We grabbed a hydrant on Mustang Drive and cooled the trees. Three Edmonton fire trucks, a department rescue truck and another crew of ten guys joined us, stretching large-volume lines into every backyard.

It was a miracle that it had taken the fire this long to hit Prairie Creek; it was closest to where MWF-009 had started, and was the first neighbourhood to receive evacuation orders. Apparently, not everyone had gotten them. Four civilians pointed on their porch and gawked at the fire as we rolled in. There wasn't time to stop and talk with them. If the worst natural disaster in Canadian history wasn't convincing enough, what reason did I have to think a stern talking-to would make them move? The best bet was to fight and keep the fire from them. They cheered us on while we swamped their backyards and bushes.

Everyone did their part, and with the probies picking up steam, I got into the trees with them. "Hey, Damian," called Greg Raymond, a former FMFD firefighter who'd since moved to Edmonton. "What are you doing?"

"Fightin' fire," I yelled back.

He walked thirty feet into the trees towards me. "With that?"

I looked down at the garden hose in my hands. "It was all that was available."

"Gotta do your part," he said. "It's good to see you again. Wish it was under better circumstances."

"We're gonna win this," I said. "We've got it."

I had no reason to believe otherwise. Despite the first day's disastrous start, we'd saved the vast majority of the houses in every community the fire had since touched down on. And soon we could add this subdivision to the list of triumphs. But there was no time to celebrate—the fire had pushed through to one of the most critical buildings in the community: Fort McMurray International Airport.

I helped my crew break down the lines and started packing. Before we finished racking the hose, Captain Pomeroy approached me, looking fatigued and exasperated. "Hey, man," he said. "We've been in the smoke for days. When is this going to end?"

"Us, too," I replied. "That was a long night."

Embers were crashing into the airport, lighting up a hotel, threatening other vital structures, and there was more than a little radio chatter calling for help. "I'm on my way out there now. If you wanna take that, I'll watch this." "I'll stay here," he said. "I'm already hooked to the hydrant." We pulled off the corner with Pat Duggin's crew and raced to the airport.

That a city of 80,000 to 125,000 (depending on who you do or don't count) would have an international airport gives you a pretty good idea of how vital Fort McMurray is to the world.

But during the first week of May 2016, the airport runways were playing a far more essential role as the hub of water bombers protecting our city.

Since Sunday, the airport's helicopter pads and private runways had buzzed frenetically, with twelve-minute turnarounds for the tankers carrying loads of red retardants. Eight minutes to reload, four to take off. The second one plane departed, the next one landed. Mother Nature had humbled twenty of the country's best aerial firefighters, but there was no reason to give up—even if the flames had landed on the Chateau Nova Hotel, just 1.5 kilometres away.

A ladder truck was the first on site. Our truck and Duggin's arrived soon after the front lobby archway caught fire. The sign's yellow N gave out, dangling on the overhang and dropping with a clang. All around me, bushes were crowning and pushing east to Saprae. I am not a religious man, but something like a prayer came over me, wishing for another erratic wind change that would nudge the fire southeast, where there were no communities. Until then, I had reality to deal with.

"Don't worry about this," Duggin told me before I stepped out. "There's something burning badly by the terminal. Give them a hand. We'll hold this."

We raced to a structure fire that was flinging embers at the terminal building, the Alberta Forestry building and the airport's private fire hall. Captain Max Cowan's crew had a "master" stream off their truck monitor and "solid" streams from the hand lines, which were anything but masterful or solid. The pressure was so weak, but it wasn't the system's fault this time; their pumper was stretched to the nearest hydrant, three hundred feet away.

There's a law of dynamics to consider in firefighting called Friction Loss: $FL = CQ^2L$. That's the coefficient for hose diameter (15.5 for a 45mm attack line) times the flow rate in litres per minute—squared—times the length of hose. Some people think firefighting is all about strength, but there's a lot of physics to the job. And the equation in this particular scenario was telling us the pumper couldn't possibly create enough pressure from hydrants a football field away. On flames this hot, you want the shortest, widest hose, which we could pull off with one of the best tricks of the trade.

"You can't pump this," I told Cowan. "Take your crew straight to the fire. We'll go to the hydrant and relay to you."

The firefighters turned to each other with furrowed eyebrows, mouthing "Relay?" Did they think I was going to make them run buckets of water like a race baton? Thankfully, Hitchcock was there to school them.

"What we're going to do is essentially turn our truck into a hydrant," he explained, backing up Pumper 310 while Max's crew drove forwards. I stayed back to observe the fire movement, now splaying across the flat roof.

"Use the high-volume pony," Kyle continued, referring to a six-foot-long, hundred-millimetre hose. "It's going to take in as much water to our pump as it can, then our pump is going to speed it up, and we're passing it to the next pumper through a three-hundred-foot high-pressure hose—with a big boost of pressure. Then they'll have enough pressure to supply their attack lines. Make sense?" He parked the pumper, opened his door and turned around to their blank stares. "C'mon, let's go!"

They scrambled to the back cabin. Pellegrin and another firefighter manned the three-hundred-footer, while Heikel pulled the pony to the hydrant and had it connected to the pumper. But nothing happened. Was the hydrant suddenly tapped?

"Guys!" yelled Hitchcock. "That's an outlet—hook the hydrant to an inlet." They switched the connections and we were in action, spraying the flames for almost an hour until they were knocked down and it was just a matter of cooling it down. "You're good here," I told Max. "You don't need a lot of water."

We drove to the hotel, which was now a lost cause. The fire had entered through the roof, sweeping through the hotel's 170 units like deranged housekeeping. Without enough respirator masks to go around for every crew, we choked on the heavy, toxic smoke swarming us. On the eastern tip of Airport Road, an intense ground fire in the woods was coming close to hangars at Wood Buffalo Helicopter, threatening the aerial firefighters' apparatus and infrastructure. Their twelve-bedroom crew house was already burning. Incredibly, the pilots and maintenance guys continued their aerial attacks, even while their quarters, industrial buildings and scrap metal and scrap wood sites caught fire around them.

We were at the hotel for two hours, but there was little we could do but try to contain the inferno to one disaster. I stood with Pat Duggin, staring down a wall of fire, watching the corners of the hotel cave. Beyond it, in the bushes, the plume crept ever more easterly.

"Damian, man, it's pushing out to your place."

"Yeah, I know." I also knew Saprae's volunteer firefighters were still deployed in Fort McMurray, leaving the hamlet indefensible until someone redeployed firefighters there. At the moment, we were stretched thin out here, on Airport Road, in Gregoire, downtown and in Wood Buffalo and Timberlea, where the Beast had returned to the two northwest neighbourhoods we fought yesterday and threatened to invade Birchwood Trails—terrorizing 60 percent of the city's homes. I didn't have to be a battalion chief or deputy to know what was priority number one.

"Why don't you grab your crew and go?" asked Pat.

"There's nothing one crew can do in that dead-end road," I said numbly. "There's no chance."

"You've gotta try. Go ahead."

I thought about it: Should I pack up the crew, head to Evergreen Place, soak the home I built for my family? How would that look to the department? To the public? The fire captain's house still standing in a devastated neighbourhood—would I ever live that down?

The radio hissed with Captain Allen Vanderkratch's voice. "We're losing Stonecreek," he said with panic. "We need any available man-power on Stonecreek!"

I wiped sweat off my forehead and rubbed my eyes. "All right," I hollered to my crew, clapping for their attention. "We're headed back to the city."

PART THREE

TAMING THE BEAST

CHAPTER 9

THE BATTLE OF BIRCHWOOD TRAILS

The Battle of Birchwood Trails began on Tower Road and in McKinlay on day one of the fire, but it did not end there. We won those fights, but around midday on May 4, temperatures rose, humidity dropped and the fuel became volatile in an effect known as crossover that gave both fires another breath. Smoulders on Tower Road flared up, despite the Fort McKay and Saprae crews' best efforts, and blew east through the live trees towards the gully leading right into the precious parkland. Some three hundred houses lined the perimeter, all of them crowned with the same cedar-shake roofs. The wood shingles serve no particular purpose other than aesthetic pleasure . . . unless you're the Beast. In that case, they're a five-kilometre trail of kindling guiding you to Birchwood Trails.

At the same time, the crossover blew up the fires outside the McKinlay trailers. The flames curled around Timberlea's northwestern perimeter into a new development, Parsons Creek, where they scorched two schools under construction and then continued over a wooded path that divides Parsons Creek from Timberlea and splays into a dense residential zone at the top of the hill.

Battalion Chief Mike Woykin was in charge of the quadrant, which stretched from the juncture of Tower Road and Birchwood Trails all the way to the other side of Timberlea. "At all costs," ADC Butz told Battalion Chief Woykin, "we have to make sure it doesn't get into Birchwood Trails."

Woykin ordered heavy equipment operators to clear half a kilometre of timber, creating a massive firebreak that they soaked with millions of litres of water. It was only half the battle. Wicked winds propelled embers over the guard and onto the roofs, decks and lawns of Walnut Crescent, where a number of gardens were landscaped with decorative wood chips, offering the flames a racetrack to the vinyl siding. The coin-sized embers morphed into monsters that devoured structures in under ten minutes each.

While we were in Gregoire that afternoon, Pitchers's crew had been redeployed there. He worked with Nathan Cseke's squad truck to douse the flames as they landed in the decorative mulch. They held it to nine houses, largely with garden hoses. At the northern greenbelt across the crescent, Cseke directed crash trucks to spray the trees with their turret nozzles, while dozers bravely pushed back the tree line. The brush fire kept flaring up, getting too close for comfort. Cseke directed a wild land crew from Alberta Forestry to help with the blizzard of embers. "I need you to put those out. Get across the street and stay there."

"You already have a crew there," he said.

"I know that, but the crash trucks are holding the trees, so I need you over there to make sure there's no embers flaring up."

The whole Forestry crew headed into the bush behind the homes to assist the firefighters with stomping out the hot spots.

Now Cseke had another problem on his hands: a dozer had gotten stuck in the blazing bush. The driver was trapped inside while trees candled around him and fire encircled his machine. Cseke ran over to a crash truck captain. "I need all your water, relocate it at the dozer."

"Are you serious?" If an ARFF's ultra-powered cannon could tear eaves off houses, it almost certainly would knock a guy out cold.

"Spray it down so we can get him out!"

Cseke's heart was racing. The flames were just inches from the dozer track, six feet high and licking the machinery with the wind. The truck revved up, taking a deep breath before yelling at the top of its lungs. If this didn't work, and if it didn't drown the fire, the operator would have to bail and make a run for it through the fire. "Duck down," yelled Cseke. The crash nozzle erupted in a long and piercing scream and blasted the burning bush with so much force the dozer almost tipped over. The operator poked his head in the window. The burning bush was smouldering. But the driver wouldn't get out—not without his machinery. He rocked it back and forth until he was free.

Across the street, Woykin made a tactical decision to lose three houses to protect dozens more. Firefighters and medics chased spot fires with garden hoses. Two urban firefighting crews set defensive perimeters protecting houses on both ends of the road. A Syncrude captain arrived in a crash truck.

"You've got foam on board?" Woykin asked. The industry captain nodded yes. "I need you to make it look like Christmas."

"What?"

"I need you to spray the exposures of the houses across the street, front and back. Make it look like Christmas."

Within minutes, a low-viscosity white liquid covered the block, buying the crews precious time. But once again, nature had other ideas. The wind picked up, flinging embers almost a kilometre farther into the west side of Birchwood Trails. The battalion chief phoned Butz immediately.

"Listen," said Woykin, standing at the edge of the trails. "I've got spot fires in the park. I've got crews on them with piss-packs and shovels, and I'm going to get a recon further into the bush to see what's going on. I'm just letting you know."

The conversation was brief, but Butz called him back minutes later. "I've got bombers coming your way."

"Serious? Jody, they're just spot fires."

"We need a preemptive strike."

> The wind picked up, flinging embers almost a kilometre farther into the west side of Birchwood Trails.

Until then, the fight within the town itself was being waged from the ground, but Birchwood Trails, being a forest within the community, forced us to go aerial. Woykin waited for the "bird dogs"—twin-engine Turbo Commander aircraft that spot the area and mark the targets for the water bombers carrying twelve-thousand-litre loads of retardant and requiring special pilots to drop them on targets with military precision. They fly in packs, coming quickly with an ear-stinging buzz and warbling siren and then disappearing as quickly as they arrived. But after ten minutes, there was no sign of them.

Woykin called Butz back. "What's going on?"

"Are the planes there yet?" Butz asked urgently.

"Negative, don't see any planes."

"You sure?"

"Don't hear 'em, don't see 'em."

"They ain't there yet?"

"Yeah, nope—oh, wait."

A bird dog suddenly loomed over the urban parkland to spot the fire, flying just above the canopies, chirping its alarms to clear ground crews. But even after the crews scrambled into the residential area, the bombers passed over them without dropping a load.

Butz called Woykin back. "The smoke's too thick. He doesn't know where to send the tankers."

"Okay," said Woykin, unsure what to do in this scenario—it had essentially become a high-level forestry operation beyond his decades of training.

"We've only got enough fuel for two more passes," explained Butz. Woykin didn't know what to say.

"Well, give 'em a target," said the assistant deputy.

"What?"

"I said, give 'em a target!"

Woykin had to think fast. "Okay," he yelled to his men. "Target, target, target!"

"Get helmets, get helmets!" Jody directed.

Woykin tossed his white helmet into the trees and black helmets followed. Some tumbled back down, so the crew there tossed them repeatedly until they stuck in the branches. But it still wasn't obvious enough for the pilot. The bird dog flew over fast, leaving the ground crew with gut-wrenching fear. Just one pass left to go. Do or die.

"You *need* to make a target for these guys," ordered Jody. "I can't stress this enough—it has to be big and bright."

"I need targets!" Woykin called to everyone in earshot. Someone thought quickly, yanking a rescue blanket off the truck. Two by two metres and decorated with the Regional Municipality of Wood Buffalo crest, it's rarely touched unless we have survivors on the side of a highway crash, freezing in the night. More important, it's bright red.

"Get that into the middle of the bushes," said Woykin, as he and the firefighter pulled the blanket by the corner three hundred feet into the trails. "I want it right there. Angle it for me—angle it, so he can get a good target!"

The bird dog returned, buzzing and chirping louder as it flew even lower, followed by a flock of bombers with open chutes— *BANG BANG BANG BANG*. They hit their target in a combination punch, covering the area with a red retardant that extinguished the little spot fires and protected the forest against any more spot fires.

> The bird dog returned, buzzing and chirping louder as it flew even lower.

It was a huge triumph and a big morale booster, but with so many eyes on Birchwood Trails, Tower Road and Walnut Crescent, Woykin and his many men couldn't see what was happening out west, on the other side of Timberlea. Near the subdivision of Prospect Pointe, at the base of a treed hill beneath Parsons Creek, the fire was preparing a second-front attack on Birchwood Trails. Thankfully, two firefighters were about to spot the new danger.

Curtis Robinson and Garrett Hovagimian, who work for me on A-shift, were officially assigned as medics during the fire, but they quickly became floaters as there was no medical work, just firefighting—jumping from pumper to pumper, regardless of whether it was with the Fort McMurray Fire Department or an out-of-town truck. They badly wanted to be on the front lines, protecting their city, however they could.

They'd spent the afternoon of Wednesday, May 4, in Thickwood, protecting the water treatment plant from embers. It was a dicey and heavy battle; at one point, a massive grass fire was fifty metres from the front door, and inside, Jette instructed his team to gather life preservers and open the main gate to the river; they'd even soaked piles of towels in case they needed to cover their faces while running into the high-velocity river. Who knows where it would have taken them. Thankfully, they didn't find out, and once they were in the clear, the firefighters were called back to Mac Island in the evening for redeployment.

Staging was more orderly at that point. There were toiletries and clean clothes for quick showers, and more cots for resting. A proper kitchen there wasn't, but logistics had gathered some barbecues in the parking lot and asked the left-behind civilians, even street folks, to volunteer cooking thousands of burgers. One homeless guy was so dedicated to feeding us he'd burned his hands in the grill fire.

That was the good news. The bad news was that staging was controlling the rest times for firefighters. They knew that, without those controls, every firefighter would be out in the field all the time. Robinson and Hovagimian were put in a queue. The pumper they'd arrived in would have to sit there until the truck ahead moved up a spot, and the next, and the next, until theirs was the first-line truck, when they would then be redeployed. The intentions were good: Can-TF2 and Incident Command wanted to give guys working ten uninterrupted hours' time to rest and refuel. But Robinson and Hovagimian were eager to get back out, unable to just sit there while their city burned.

There were so many guys ahead of them, they knew it would be a while before they would get back out there. Robinson had a home near Prospect Pointe and had heard chatter about Woykin's epic battle not far from it. After only a few minutes—enough time to guzzle some water and scarf a burger—the boys decided to take the opportunity to head to their homes and change clothes. They then drove towards the northeast side of Timberlea in Robinson's personal SUV.

Turning left from Highway 63 onto Confederation Way, they spotted smoke billowing from a hillside above an industrial park, close to

Prospect Pointe. Not only was the fire threatening the subdivision on the west but it was also pushing up the hill from the east, both fronts closing in on Stonecreek Landing and Gravelstone Road. They pulled a U-turn, returned fast to Mac Island and reported it to Hanson. The staging officer repaid them by plunking them in the queue again. "Guys have to rest," he said.

> Every region of Alberta was represented by at least one man or woman in those streets and bushes.

They were desperate to get back out there. They didn't have to wait long. At the front of the queue, a pumper from Olds, Alberta, seven hundred kilometres south of Fort McMurray, was being deployed to Sandstone Lane in Prospect, and two more could squeeze into the back cab.

The Olds crew didn't know Sandstone Lane from Limestone Link or Shalestone Way or Gravelstone Road, so Robinson and Hovagimian helped guide them along the way. The boys directed the truck to the right place, where Captain Allen Vanderkratch—or AVK, as he's known—needed them.

As they set up hoses to keep the fire out of the crescent—and out of Stonecreek Village Mall behind them, and Limestone Link Park behind that, and the cluster of houses leading into Birchwood Trails behind it all—more resources arrived and spread through Prospect. It was practically a firefighting conference; every region of Alberta was represented by at least one man or woman in those streets and bushes. Even the town's fire marshal straddled a hose on the battlefield.

Crews at the bottom of the hill couldn't keep the fire in the trees. The firestorm intensified and created a southwestern wind blowing thousands of embers into the community. Crews raced under the sky of fire, trying to soak houses with water and foam, stomp out hot spots on decks and blow them away on roofs. That's when AVK radioed for help.

Pumper 310 had now done a near 360-degree tour of the city over the course of thirty hours. From the southwestern tip of Beacon Hill, northwest to Wood Buffalo, then the whole southern and southeastern edges of Gregoire and Prairie Creek. Now we found ourselves driving to the northeastern tip. The poor truck was having a hard time, kicking out black smoke from the exhaust pipe, leaving an acrid odour trailing through Confederation Way behind us. We were working it to the bone. The old thing was still chugging along, though. We raced to Prospect, then slowed to a crawl when the smoke thickened. The sun was up, but it was almost impossible to see through the black smoke. Multiple fire trucks along the edges of the neighbourhood were working to hold back house fires on Prospect Drive.

"Captain Vanderkratch, where do you need me?" I radioed.

"Let's meet face-to-face at the Petro Canada," he replied.

When we pulled into the lot, it was the first time I had seen AVK since the start of the fire. We greeted with a short hug. Everyone was overworked and exhausted, but we were all grateful for the way we were working together. Every time crews met each other during the battle, there were hugs and handshakes, each person thankful for what others were doing and ready to embrace their fellow firefighters over what we had seen and what was still to come.

"The store is open; the owner stayed behind to help," AVK said. "Tell your crew to grab what they need. It looks like it's going to be a long night."

I waved Hitchcock over and told him the news. "Tell the crew to grab me something."

The crew entered the store while Vanderkratch and I went over the map.

"I need you on Siltstone," AVK said. "Crews are already in deeper battling the blaze, so let's hope it doesn't make it that far."

Truck loaded and spirits lifted after our quick stop, we were on our way. I was searching half for an open hydrant, half for a pedestrian, fearing we'd accidentally maim one of our own.

"There's one," I said, pointing to an open spot on Siltstone Place, in the dead centre of the subdivision.

Kyle parked the 310. "Come on, guys!" I shouted. "You've done this tons before now. Soak the houses, take a position." They pulled hand lines through a bike trail and started soaking the backs of grey vinyl-sided two-storeys separated from sixteen red row houses by a curving back alley.

There was a truck on every corner, from the west side of Prospect Drive to the east side of Gravelstone Road, and hoses dragged across every sidewalk along the Craftsman-style houses, eight-plexes and a big brown apartment building. All of it had been built within the last six years at a breakneck pace, so the buildings were clustered together, with as little as eight feet between the foundations and four feet between the eaves. We were to be a back line of defence should the fire keep pushing up the hill from Stonecreek Landing.

In the valley, dozers frantically tore live black spruce from the ground, sending thunderous rumbles through the earth with each fall. A firebreak, they hoped, would keep the wall of flames from reaching the residences en masse, and ultimately keep this a spot fire battle instead of another major defensive-attack firefight like Beacon Hill's.

"Go get the ground monitor," I told a firefighter.

He returned minutes later, pale-faced. "Uh, Captain?"

"What's up?"

"I have no idea where it is."

"Huh?"

"The ground monitor. It's not on the pump."

I started tearing apart the truck. There were garden hoses, helmets, piss-packs, empty oxygen tanks and dirty coveralls scattered about the cab, and misplaced shovels, hand-nozzles, axes and nozzles in the cabinets. But no ground monitor.

"Hitchcock, you got the ground monitor?" I asked.

"No, Cap."

"Pellegrin, Heikel—where'd you last see the monitor?"

Nobody even remembered touching it. How could we have a hardware store of garden hose handles, but not one of the costliest and most essential resources for this fight on board?

I walked from truck to truck, looking for a spare monitor. Hitchcock stayed behind, closely listening to Pumper 310. With hundreds of feet of hand lines connected to it, her engine vibrated and shook, in a way I'd never heard before in my fifteen years. Smoke billowed from the exhaust. It rocked on its wheels, making a horrible pounding noise like *knack knack knack knack*. The exhaust was denser than anything coming out of houses in the valley below. I ran towards it. Feet away, I heard metal gears rattling inside and then—*BOOM!*

The floodlights shut off. The water streams disappeared into drips. The awful noise stopped. Hitchcock and I stared at each other dumbly. The firefight froze as everyone within sight turned towards us.

"Let it cool for twenty minutes, then fire it back up," I told Hitchcock.

"Think that'll work?"

"I don't know. This wasn't in any manual."

The firefighters roved around, assisting however they could, mostly helping crews pack as they repositioned down Siltstone Place to soak every house on the block. Meanwhile, Kyle stood by 310, counting to twenty minutes and then starting it up again. The floodlights sparked to life, but so did the terrible grinding, rocking, stinking. It was time to put it out of its misery.

"I should've been more careful," Hitchcock said guiltily. He's an experienced pump operator, so he took it to heart. But none of us had ever worked a truck this hard. I doubted there was anything he could have done differently.

"Better back it up so we can get another in place," I said. He shut off the ignition for a few minutes while the grunts disconnected the hoses and left them where they lay. Kyle backed the truck up thirty feet. I radioed staging.

"My truck is done."

"What?" Hanson, still commanding Mac Island, asked in disbelief.

"The engine's done."

"Done?"

"It's done. The fire's coming at us. I need another truck."

"We'll send one," said Steve.

"We're on Siltstone."

While Hitchcock directed the crew to disconnect all our hoses, Captain Duggin called on the radio. "Yeah, go ahead," I said.

"I just finished with the airport. I'm coming up to your location to take over, so where do you need me?"

I gave him our position and told him the plan: "All our hoses are laid and waiting for you." I paused. "Is anybody in Saprae?" He was silent. "Pat—"

"Damian. I don't know."

Wed, May 3, 11:54 PM

Are you in saprae

No

Is anyone in saprae

Freaking out

By midnight on May 4, the Beast had grown to ten thousand hectares, with its limbs stretching almost the whole perimeter of the city—and beyond. Gregoire Lake Estates and Anzac, a town forty kilometres away, were mandatorily evacuated as flames sprinted south. Worse yet, Anzac's volunteer firefighters, like Saprae Creek's, were still deployed in Fort McMurray itself. Nobody could blame Travis Cramer, their volunteer fire chief, for redeploying his sixteen men and three trucks back home, where the residents were understandably miffed that they'd been left exposed. "If we don't get back there, our community will never forgive us," he told the other firefighters. They lost twelve of two hundred and fifty structures.

Southeast of me, some thirty kilometres away, a steady glow hovered over Saprae Creek, occasionally flashing high in the sky, probably whenever the flames hit a propane tank. Or a house. Darren Clarke, one of our members and the volunteer fire chief for Saprae, had tried to drive a truck there earlier that evening but didn't quite make it to the turnoff. A forty-foot high wall of fire blew across the road from one side of the bush to the other. He couldn't see around or over it, and he definitely couldn't get through it.

> MWF-009 was now so big you could see it from space.

From a spark in the grass, MWF-009 was now so big you could

see it from space. But way down here, on Planet Earth, along Siltstone Place, it was pitch-black but for the trucks' floodlights, a few house lights left on and a crescent moon playing hide-and-seek behind the dark plume wafting from the house fires in front of us. Our crew worked off Pat Duggin's truck, a spry Pierce that took the position of Pumper 310. Hitchcock set up the truck with Duggin's operator, Nathan Gilchrist, while Duggin and I discussed the strategy. "This'll be a good spot for a stand," I said. "No matter what, I think we'll be able to hold it here. We've got a back alley and a natural break in the road."

"Yup," agreed Duggin. "It's a strong defensive line."

As we waited for battle, I ordered my crew to check the nearby houses. "Make sure everyone is out," I said. "Check the yards, grab sprinklers, prepare for embers."

Just about all the crews did the same thing, trying doorknobs, jumping fences and opening gates for easy access. As we worked, more trucks staged on every corner. It turned into something out of a zombie apocalypse movie: "We've got Cheerios, what've you got?" "Oranges. Let's trade." It was a healthy morale booster.

Somewhere in the subdivision, out of view from me, Hitchcock ran into Jamieson, Relph and Shantz. Best friends in and out of the field, they'd formed their own brigade after reuniting that morning in McKinlay. Hitchcock didn't know it yet, but Relph officially learned that his house in Abasand was gone. His fiancée Sherianne's teaching modules for work, gone. Their photo albums, gone. Carey Price jersey, never to be ogled again. But he didn't mention it to Hitchcock. Relph just took an energy bar, hugged and thanked his friend and returned to work.

He wasn't alone in the department. More than a dozen firefighters were left homeless in those first thirty-six hours, whether they knew it or not.

Scott Germain, a twenty-nine-year-old acting captain and multigenerational firefighter—his twin brother, older brother, dad and uncle had all been in the field at some point in their lives—had lost his house just a few blocks from where I stood. He learned the news from his wife, a dispatcher, took a few seconds to process it, then returned to saving the city. A couple days later, he would finally break down after logging onto Facebook and seeing a photo of his twin, Jamie, in the middle of trying to douse Scott's house, even though it was well beyond the point of saving.

Judith Iwaszkiw, a dispatcher who'd never held a hose until that week, watched her backyard catch fire in Beacon Hill on her way to work on day one. It was the last time she'd see her home. When she finally returned, the brick building had turned to dust, and all that survived was a patch of lilies and the FMFD belt buckle she had forgotten to wear.

Bo Cooper had just returned to his wife, dog and king-sized bed after months of hospitalization, undergoing an experimental treatment for leukemia in the U.S. Bo, twenty-six, the son of Captain Rob Cooper and a part-time mixed-martial-arts fighter, wasn't well enough to wrestle the fire, but he rallied us through social media. I was devastated to learn he'd lost his house, just days before his welcome-home party and first wedding anniversary.

At about one in the morning my phone buzzed with a message from our home security company, notifying me that our garage door was damaged. And then it buzzed again with a message from Melanie.

> Oh wow. Sickening to think how much we lost

> We don't know for sure. Could be just the garage or smoke

Was it blind optimism? Maybe, but more than anything I just didn't have the time to consider the worst. And I kept reminding myself that, actually, it was not the worst. I was alive, and so were my brothers and sisters in the field. Melanie, Aidan and Taya were okay. Danielle, Mom, my niece, nephews and brother-in-law—all safe.

Tragically, not everyone could say that.

"Sorry about your chief," a firefighter from Lac La Biche said to me after I put my phone away.

"What's that?" I asked, my voice cracking from all the shouting and toxic air of the last thirty-six hours.

"There was a car crash by our town."

"I—" I coughed. "I know the one."

"They're saying it was your chief's daughter."

"The chief doesn't have a daughter."

"Well, one of your chiefs," he said. "I'm sorry we couldn't be there for her."

I asked around the trucks for more information. The girl was Emily Ryan, the daughter of Cranley Ryan, a Saprae volunteer deputy fire chief and the deputy chief of training with FMFD. A good friend; I'd even been to his wedding, and more than a few times to his house two streets over. Emily was a triplet. Cranley's nephew Aaron Hodgson died in the crash too.

The news gave me some perspective as the night went on, and I walked the streets for a lay of the land. Water was getting scarce. Crews were stealing water from each other's hydrants, setting up their monitor and streaming with good head pressure, which would cause the arc of another crew's monitor on the other side of the road to break short and fall.

I limped down the bike trail into an alley curving between Silt-stone Place and the red row houses. North of that, on Stonecreek Landing, crews were battling as the wind pushed the fire through the houses. There were four streets on the upper side and four on the bottom, with two apartments in the middle, fire on every street and large crews battling, trying to stop the advancing fire pushing our way. If a house became damaged beyond repair, we couldn't battle the blaze. At that point, all we could do was eliminate the fuel in front of it. Heavy machinery knocked houses to the ground to keep the fires from spreading.

The big yellow bulldozers were fourteen feet tall, weighed thousands of pounds and could shove a single detached house two feet back at fifteen kilometres per hour. But while they were powerful, they weren't all that precise. I watched as a dozer driver pushed too hard at the side of one house, shifting the building two feet off the foundation, leaving an opening into the basement. The driver didn't mind the gap, jolting forwards again. The blade plowed into the wall with a massive crunch, exposing a brightly decorated nursery room. The dozer's tracks crossed over the opening to the basement, tilting the monster forwards in slow motion as firefighters, police and paramedics yelped at each other to get out of the way.

The bulldozer toppled into the basement with a thunderous crash. A quarter of the house tumbled in after it, bringing a baby crib, dining table and granite island into the pit, along with the attic, which was still on fire. By sheer luck, the debris didn't collapse on the cab where the driver sat, but the flames only had more fuel now and spread towards him. It was utter chaos.

"Can you see him?"

"Is he alive?"

"Somebody get him!"

The driver kicked open the caged door, lifting himself out of the dozer with a gasp, like he was buried alive. He climbed onto the vehicle's track pads, then onto the flaming shingles, and reached up to four men crouching over the pit, who lifted him to safety.

"We've got to get it out," said the driver, a young guy not so overcharged on adrenaline that he didn't worry about million-dollar machinery (or what his boss would do when he found out). "Who's got chains?" They tried to rescue the machine from the pit by towing it on the back of a bigger dozer, but the fire was gaining. Eventually, they had to surrender it to the flames.

The bulldozer toppled into the basement with a thunderous crash.

The sacrifices of these private contractors were incredible. We firefighters sign up for this—maybe not anything of this scale, but it's our duty nonetheless. The contractors and water tank drivers? This dozer guy who risked his life? They all could've been with their families if they wanted, but they'd stayed behind and even come from other communities, driving into the inferno like us to help however they could.

We continued to build firebreaks and douse houses, trying to get ahead of the fires along Prospect Drive and Stonecreek Landing, but no matter what we did, it was clear that we couldn't get ahead of the flames. Crews would try to remove a building two houses away, then three or four, but the fire defied every attempt. With water pressure tapping out, crews started falling back. On the east side, fire started cruising in from the Gravelstone Road houses, threatening to ride the westerly winds up a hill of houses towards us. Half a dozen ladder trucks sprayed the roofs along Gravelstone, keeping them as moist as possible, but if the other first line of defence failed, there was no reason to think this one couldn't, too. Something drastic needed to be done.

We had to start thinking more defensively to win against this fire. When forest fighters are battling a blaze, they build wide firebreaks through the trees to try to stop the flames. Maybe that would be our solution.

The decision was made: a wider firebreak needed to be created, and my crew was in the perfect location to make it happen. The back alley in front of us had garages on either side, squeezed between two-storey houses and a street on the fire side, and there was a pipeline below us to the valley with a natural reserve area below it. It was the best spot to create the break.

The wind was in my face, blowing hard towards me; the fire was almost at my location. I eyed the row houses—untouched, unscathed homes, full of treasured possessions, irreplaceable heirlooms, joyful memories. Did we really have to do this? With crews pulling back and the fire intensifying, it was clear it had to be done.

"Butz," I heaved.

"Damian? You okay?" asked the assistant deputy.

"I'll need more bulldozers," I squeezed out.

"There are dozers up there already," Jody replied. He was overwhelmed by too many battlefronts.

"I see them. But I need more."

CHAPTER 10

CREATIVE DESTRUCTION

My whole adult life has been about home. Building it. Protecting it. Building made me better at protecting, and protecting made me better at building. Between the two, I'd dedicated everything to helping hundreds of my neighbours create or continue their happy memories in this city we love. Now I was about to put an end to them. Tear them down. Crush them. Turn them into piles of wood, steel and stone. All to save hundreds more homes in Timberlea, and tens of thousands more encircling Birchwood Trails. We're trained to fight for every home as though it were our own, but were one of these mine, would I be willing to tear it down as collateral damage? I couldn't answer. All I knew was, if the plan didn't work, I'd never forgive myself.

Firefighters pried and axed open doors to make sure the garages were empty. While they did that, we took chainsaws to back fences to pull them out of the way.

"Cap, the garages are full—trucks, cars, quads, skidoos. What do we do?"

"Check the houses, see if there are keys to drive them out of the way."

While firefighters cleared garages, Hitchcock rushed between backyards, yanking propane tanks from every barbecue and moving them to the front. After clearing a dozen barbecues in as many minutes, Hitchcock paused and dropped the propane tank he was holding on the lawn. He was soaking wet in his coveralls. He'd slept just three hours over nearly two days, and I knew from how dazed I was that he felt the same. But he didn't stop.

"Cap, there's no keys. Should we move them by hand?"

I scanned the street to examine the fire. It had advanced three more houses in the time we had looked for keys. I wanted to say yes, that we had to do everything we could. But just then, the two hulking, yellow dozers arrived in the alley.

"We don't have time," I explained.

I approached the dozer guys standing in front of their blades, wearing masks. "Start with the backs. Take out the decks, garages, sheds. Just level it. Push everything down into the valley. Any debris catches, my guys are standing by to put it out."

"How long you think we got?" asked a driver. On the west side, along Prospect Drive, it was burning fifteen houses away. Down the east hill, the fire breached the tree line, roaring like an oncoming jet engine, while firefighters sprayed water from the sides to try to keep it at bay.

"An hour," I said.

"That's impossible," he said.

"We've got to try. I'll try to get us more dozers, but right now you're all we've got. We'll move to the houses next if we need to flatten them out." They nodded, tightened their hard hats and stepped inside the caged cabs. "All right," I called over the fire with my cracked voice, "we're doing this!" All around me, I heard colleagues shouting "Clear the way!" to one another. I radioed Vanderkratch. "I have the dozers in position. We're starting the break."

"Will it work?" he asked.

"I sure hope so." How could I live with myself if it didn't?

The dozers rolled forwards, weakening the structures' corners first to avoid the same mistake as the last guy. Then they hit them with such force that the buildings slid off their foundations. Grey and white corrugated siding cracked on impact, falling off the blades' edges as the dozers reversed. They pounced forwards again, punching open garage walls and exposing strangers' private lives through their motorcycles, ATVs and children's bicycles. It was heart-wrenching but necessary. The dozers pushed ahead, turning hundreds of thousands of dollars of assets and priceless memories into collateral damage for the greater good. Car alarms rang over the crunching, as corners of walls gave out and caved in on themselves.

Two smaller dozers arrived, Cats without much force but a lot of claw. "Start pushing that debris down the hill," I told the drivers. "Get rid of all of it. Widen the firebreak as much as you can."

The dozers rolled the debris across the alley and down the hill, into a path that had already been cleared of trees. If it weren't for the firefighters tucked between the houses, soaking each pile as it was pushed downhill, you'd swear I was a foreman in a construction zone.

I coordinated the dozing, while Hitchcock took captain's duties and coordinated the firefighters. "Get in deeper," I heard him shout to Heikel, Pellegrin and a dozen others. "You, get in farther. Move your water streams here. Make sure you get those shingles. Great, good!"

AVK radioed me from the other side of the neighbourhood, where he was trying to get a long view of the battle. "It's ten houses from you. How are you doing? Is it going to work?"

At this point, with everyone pulled out in front of us, the fire had gained momentum and consumed the next street over. It was pushing faster in our direction, and I feared the break wasn't wide enough.

"It's got to," I replied. "We have about sixty percent cleared."

Embers were raining down on us and in the houses behind us. Duggin had crews from multiple departments three blocks deep jumping fences and climbing roofs, putting out spot fires that had begun to develop behind us.

"You keep doing what you're doing, Asher. I'll look after this."

After forty-five minutes, the water that had soaked the houses on one side of the break was drying out. The heat was starting to intensify, and the fire was climbing to Prospect Drive across the street. The one-block alley on Siltstone was cleared, but there was far more to go.

"How you doing?" I asked a driver.

"Good."

"You ready to keep goin'?"

"Yup."

I pointed to the row houses. "Think you can do it?"

"I'll give it a try."

Again, they worked the corners, trying to make the structure fall on itself like a house of cards. Behind me, a massive spotlight cast my shadow onto the demolition. It came from two track-hoes—excavators with thirty-foot reach. Shielding my eyes from the light, I marched to the cabs. One of the drivers was Kevin, a contractor who'd helped dig out my foundation in Saprae. "Something tells me this job's a little different than the last one," he joked.

"You got it," I said.

I marched back to the sidelines, threw the excavator drivers two thumbs-up and waved them in to start clawing at the structures' roofs stretching across the block.

"Five houses away," AVK squawked into the radio.

I stood in the back alley, unable to see past the wall of flames along Prospect Drive, taking AVK's word as gospel. We frantically tried to widen the path to keep the fire from getting up. Firefighters doused hot spots as embers rained down on us, hitting the ground with a thud. Some were the size of basketballs, smacking decks and roofs and lighting up debris from the destruction.

Just when I thought the situation was under control, a driver started hollering at me for help. Behind him, the fire was ten feet tall and nearing the property line of Prospect Drive. "What's wrong?" I asked.

"It's too hot, the machine's overheating. I have to stop."

I looked around—there were four guys on every corner, hosing the debris. "Bring it over here," I blurted to them. "Come on, come on. Move it!" Four guys jogged over, two to each hose, lugging the sopping tubes over their shoulders. "I need you keep their machines cool." Staying a few paces behind, they sprayed the excavators, stepping forwards and backwards as the tracks reversed and accelerated.

"Five houses away."

The toppled row houses were cleared out, but four homes on the hilltop were still standing, allowing the fire to cling to their backyards and decks and whip up their sides.

I jogged to Kevin in the track-hoe. "What do you think of those houses?"

"Not a problem," he said.

He dug into their roofs and pulled them down, picking up flaming debris and turning it over onto the ground for the firefighters to extinguish. Once it was doused, bulldozers rolled in and pushed it down the hill, which was beginning to resemble a landfill.

Now it's happening, I thought to myself. *Now we're ahead of it.* We were spraying backyards, spraying debris, spraying roofs. Hot spots on decks, fences, trash cans—all short-lived, because we had dozens of men and women chasing embers with shovels and heavy-duty boots. The fire was right in front of us, but there was a huge guard it would have to leap if it wanted a taste of Siltstone Place and the rest of the neighbourhood.

AVK's voice crackled: "It looks like it's on top of you."

"Yes, it's hit the houses on the edge of the break. But we're getting ahead of it," I said. "This is going to work."

Ground monitors and hand lines doused the rubble with beautiful streams—and then, the water dropped. The arcs shrunk to a trickle. The hydrants were dead.

"Send me tankers! Send me tankers!" I yelled into the radio. "Send me water shuttles. Send me crash trucks!" All that work, so much devastation. We couldn't let it stop here. We had to keep fighting.

> In the minutes before the first tanker arrived, the debris fire grew fierce and was blown into the row houses' foundations, igniting more rubble.

In the minutes before the first tanker arrived, the debris fire grew fierce and was blown into the row houses' foundations, igniting more rubble. The firefighters reconnected their hand lines to the tanker, draining all ten thousand litres in under five minutes, cooling but not killing the flames.

The tanker backed up and left, and before the next one could arrive, the flames sparked up again. It continued like this for hours. Up, down, up, down. Cool, hot, cool, hot. Tanker in, tanker gone. We tried our hardest to keep up, and it was pushing us to our physical and mental limits.

The boys and girls were bagged. Some of them were fighting from lawn chairs, hosing the flames with their eyes literally closed. If they weren't fatigued, they were freezing, moving dangerously close to the flames to warm up.

"When are we pulling out?" asked a firefighter.

"We're not," I replied. "This is it. We have to stop it here. If these houses behind us light up, we just pull back four houses and keep fighting the fight. So follow me, stay close and pay attention. We'll put this fire out tonight."

Hovagimian sauntered over to me. By then, his truck from Olds had returned to staging, so he and Robinson had tagged along with our crew instead of getting stuck at Mac Island again. "I dunno, Cap," he said, distressed. "I don't know if I can keep going."

"What's wrong?" I asked.

"I'm soakin' wet. I'm freezin' cold, and all I've got are my coveralls."

"Okay," I replied. "Go back to work, and let's see what we can do."

I walked back to the first house around the corner, a two-storey suburban house with a small front porch. I tried the doorknob. It was unlocked. Leaving a trail of mud up the stairs, I checked every bedroom closet for clothes. I found dresses, blouses, lacy shawls, a teenager's bubblegum-bright sweaters, snowboarding jackets that would hardly fit Aidan. I figured a single mom and her two girls lived there. It was more of the same in the basement's spare room, as I tugged at dresser drawers. Finally, I lucked out, prying open a closet full of men's clothing. I grabbed all the sweaters I could and returned to the war zone with a bundle of clothes.

I tossed one at Hovagimian, another at Robinson, and so on. "Here's a sweater for you. Here's a sweater for you." I was the crews' Oprah Winfrey, giving away clothes to guys who were happier to own a new sweater than a new car. They wiggled out of their shirts, let the tops of their coveralls drape over their legs, slid into drier clothes and picked up their hand lines to get right back to work.

Soon, the debris was almost all cleared, leaving a manageable bonfire. But the foundations smouldered, and the wind hadn't subsided at all, so we needed to keep a close eye on it.

I gathered a few firefighters, some dozen guys from a variety of crews. "The door's open," I said, pointing to the house. "The house is safe, and you'll be close to the action if you're needed. Find a bed if you can, get some sleep, then get back and switch out with someone." Within minutes, it turned into a squat house. A motley crew of firefighters, paramedics and EMTs spread across three floors, crawling into a little girl's bed, onto a sofa or any chunk of floor they could find. Grown men and women—dirty, stinky, haven't-showered-in-days adults—collapsed side by side, still in full bunker gear.

It must have filled up fast. On the same block, a couple of guys found another unlocked door. Heikel, shivering cold, and another dozen firefighters immediately flooded in, stomping around in dirty boots, raiding the kitchen and tossing their wet clothes in the dryer. They could not have picked a more obsessively compulsive home-owner; the cans in the pantry were aligned in perfect order with labels facing outwards, including one that said coffee. It was emptied almost immediately.

Pellegrin slept on a couch, and Heikel folded himself at the foot of it like a dog. Us captains let them lie in the two houses for about an hour each, switching them off with the others who had been left dousing the debris. Water tenders were still coming and going, and the small dozers chipped away at the scorched fences surrounding the former houses. But too much time had passed since the last time I saw Pellegrin and Heikel on a hose line, so I shook them awake. "Come on, wake up," I said. "There's another two water tenders on the way." I turned back and walked out, but only Pellegrin followed. "Heikel—now! Grab a line!"

He limped to the doorway. "Come on, Captain. Is this it?" he asked indignantly. "Are we just going to keep doing this? Are we just going to work, work, work, no rest, no sleep, no food?"

I got it. He was tired. As was I. But we were still in the fight, and the fight wasn't over. We walked back towards the action and talked along the way.

"Look around," I said. "What are we going to do? The fire is still going, so we have to as well. I would love to have a rest, but I need you for just a few more hours, and then I will try to find you some rest after that."

Eventually, we brought the fire down to a manageable size, and the crews were able to get their well-deserved rest. Someone had dragged a brown sofa they had found in a backyard down to the edge of the break. Captain Duggin and I sat and reflected on the evening's events. We had stopped the fire from advancing through the subdivision, but what would people think about what we had done? How were the guys going to cope with what we had done? Too tired to play out the whole situation, Duggin started to doze off. I told him to join the crew in the house and get some sleep while I stayed out and kept watch, making sure everyone was safe. He accepted and wandered out of sight down the alley.

As the sun lit up the earth, I saw that the grass was scorched right to the property line of Prospect Drive. The plan had worked. We had won this battle, but I was done, in such a haze that I couldn't even think about my home in Saprae. It felt like an illusion, as if at any minute I could find myself back in bed on the Tuesday morning, long before the battle had begun, with nothing to do that day but mow my lawn and trim some hedges. Melanie was texting me but I couldn't make out the words.

I sat there, half-awake, until 9:00 a.m. With the dozers gone and the flames extinguished, I called for a flatbed to pick up Pumper 310 and the crew. "Where are ya?" asked Battalion Chief Kelly.

I looked around at rows of tall grey houses, at the smoking carnage in between. "I don't have a clue," I said. "I don't know the name of this street. I can't make up a name for this street. I can't even walk to a street sign to find out the name of this street. Just find me and take us to Mac Island."

CHAPTER 11

SECOND WIND

E very step felt like a four-hundred-pound leg press, and the doors of Mac Island looked a town away. I hobbled across the lot and into the rec centre, while a flurry of faint and muffled voices called my name—asking, I think, if I was okay. My head wasn't so much spinning as hollowed out. Nothing registered as I limped along in my waterlogged boots, before collapsing in a gap between two vending machines. My senses were wiped clean but for the pins and needles zapping my feet.

Leaning forwards, I unzipped my duty boots for the first time in two days. Water trickled to the tiles as I feebly kicked at the back heels, exposing sopping, rancid grey socks. I peeled them off tenderly, skin sloughing off with them, revealing a swollen, white, wrinkly horror show. Pigment and circulation had been sucked dry, and my big toe was as big as an apple. Bubbles of pus swished inside blisters. After two days in unsanitary, damp ground, I'd developed something like trench foot.

A familiar name managed to break through my daze. "Tia?" Steve Morari was running through the bodies, stopping every time he saw an FMFD helmet to ask for his wife. "Have you seen Tia?" he said in panic. It'd been two days since they last saw each other. He'd heard she was somewhere inside Mac Island, lost in the bodies of emergency personnel and volunteers.

"Damian—Jesus Christ," he said, stopping in front of me. "You look like you were in a building collapse."

"Hi. Steve," I mustered, looking right through him.

"Have you seen Tia? Someone said she's here." I just lifted my dead arm and pointed to a corner of the crowded hall where she was pounding back a Gatorade. Steve sprinted to her, calling her name until she noticed. They embraced with a huge hug and kiss.

I wanted to call Melanie, tell her that I loved her, that I missed her, that I wanted to be there with her and Taya and Aidan. But my phone was dead and I doubted I had the thumb strength to unlock it anyway.

"Hey, Cap," said Hitchcock, handing me a packet of Moleskin blister padding. "Put this on." Other firefighters around me were sticking these little pain relievers to their nasty feet, practically in tears as the patches eased their agony, or they were cutting dead skin off with pocketknives and duct-taping gauze over their feet.

Over the last two days, I had made sure he had a couple of hours of sleep, and now it was his turn to look out for me. "I'm done," I told Hitchcock. "I need some sleep; just a couple of hours. Then we've got to get back out and help."

"Okay, cool," he said, pulling a chair by my side.

I handed him my phone. "Charge."

"No problem."

We had been looking after each other for days. He could have taken this opportunity to go find some food, have a shower or catch up with his friends. Instead, he stayed and made sure I got some undisturbed rest. I was so thankful.

And then, for the first time in fifty-one hours, my eyes closed.

"Hey, Captain."

The voice seemed to come from inside my head.

"Hey, Captain." This time it came with a nudge to my shoulder.

I felt like I needed the Jaws of Life to open my eyes, even though I'd only been out for forty-five minutes. Lying, back flat on the floor, I stared at the blurry figure of a man I didn't recognize.

"Are you okay?" he asked.

"Yeah. I been sleeping," I replied.

"Well, you look like hell."

"Yeah," I huffed. "I been fightin' fire for three days."

"But you're okay?"

"Yeah," I said, looking behind the man and making faint eye contact with Nick Waddington, president of our union, in conversation with members of the Alberta Fire Fighters Association. The group of them approached and stood over me between the vending machines.

"We heard what happened last night in Prospect," said Nick. "You might have saved the whole community."

"I'd normally get up," I huffed. "But I can't. I can't right now."

> I felt like I needed the Jaws of Life to open my eyes.

"No problem," said Nick.

Another person crouched down beside me, asking, "How ya doing, Asher? How's your morale?"

Hitchcock, holding a pair of fresh socks, put his hand on one of their shoulders, prompting them to turn around. "Hey," said Kyle, "let the man sleep."

"Sorry," the man responded, rising from the ground. He turned back to me. "Outstanding work last night."

The firefighters threw me a thumbs-up and walked on. Kyle slid the chair in front of my feet, blocking me from view. "Fresh socks," he said, tossing a balled-up pair into my lap.

"Where am I?" I asked mid-yawn, mouth so wide my jaw cracked. "What time is it?"

"We're staged in Mac Island. Hasn't been long."

"The fire's gone?" I asked.

"Negative. But it's cooling down. They say it's gonna be nineteen degrees."

"We gotta get to work," I blurted. "Get on a pump."

"Cap, there's no pumper—310's done." Last night was a haze, but it was coming back to me now: the dense black smoke billowing from the exhaust, the knocking and grinding of the gears, the track-hoe, the dozers, the destruction. "C'mon, let's get going," I said. "We've got to get to hall 5. My truck's there, so we can go from there."

Hitchcock helped me to my feet as I struggled to get off the ground. He grabbed my arm as I hobbled to the doors, barefoot, forgetting my phone and new footwear behind. "Let's go—"

"Damian," said a voice from behind. It belonged to Tany Yao, a former paramedic and assistant deputy chief with the FMFD before he entered public office and became an Alberta member of the legislature with the Wildrose Party. He gave me a big hug and asked if I was okay.

I looked down at my hideous feet, patched in Moleskin pads, flaking like they'd been put through cheese graters. My uniform was caked with dirt, and my face was covered in stubble.

"How's your family?" asked Tany.

"Family is safe," I said.

"And the house?" I shrugged to say I didn't know. He put a sympathetic hand on my shoulder. "The whole world is rooting for you."

Brian Jean, leader of the Wildrose Party, joined our conversation. I'd also known him over the years, watched him rise from businessman to lawyer to leader of the opposition, and watched with great admiration when, a year prior, he showed incredible resilience following the death of his twenty-four-year-old son. Few politicians are as humble as Brian, and even as one of the most powerful politicians in Alberta, he wore boot-cut jeans and a camouflage sweater under his black coat. "I heard all about last night," Brian said. "You guys did incredible."

"Just doing our jobs," I replied. I remembered that Brian lived in Waterways, where all but a handful of buildings had been razed on the first day of battle. "Did your house make it?"

His lips tightened into a sad smile and started quivering. I put a comforting hand on his shoulder.

"Wish I could be there with you boys," said Tany. "Man, what a battle." He handed his phone to his assistant. "How about a group picture?"

Hitchcock rolled his eyes, slithered from the embrace. "No thank you."

"Come on—" pleaded Tany.

"No way, man. I'm not taking a photo," Hitchcock interrupted. "If you want to take a picture, go ahead, Cap."

I apologized to Tany, but I understood Kyle's reaction. We were out there working hard to save our communities, covered in soot and reeking of ash, and he didn't want to end up in a photo op. Hitchcock is passionate to a fault, and after posing for the photo, I pulled him aside. "Hey," I said, "I get it. I do. But Brian Jean lost his son last year, and now he just lost his house too, with all of his memories of his son in it. He's going through a lot right now."

"Well, shit," he said guiltily. "I didn't know that."

"We're still in the uniform, right? So we still have to represent the department well." I nodded once in a show of forgiveness. "Let's get to

> "The whole world is rooting for you guys."

hall 5, see if they've got something good to eat," I said, limping back to the stuff I'd forgotten. My feet stung as I pulled new socks over them. I picked up my boots, now at least two sizes too small for my swollen feet, grabbed the phone and charger, and looked at the screen: four missed calls from Melanie, all minutes apart. Then, a text message:

Thu, May 5, 10:25 PM

From Pam

"Your house sounds like it's safe. A guy who stored his trailer at our house was just there. Our house burnt and everything on it but the kids play set, backhoe and dump trailer right to the ground. He said everyone around is still standing. It's like a bomb was dropped just on our property alone."

Looks like ours made it

Looks like it

An ember must have crashed into Pam Garbin's roof. Without anyone there to hit the spot fires, it pulled every wall, every floor, every possession inside the earth, and turned the foundation of her beautiful two-storey custom-built home into an ashtray. All across the city we were seeing similar freak occurrences—whole blocks intact but for one house razed to smouldering ruins. It could have just as easily been our home—our photo albums, our bookshelves, our bed, our kids' toys turned to ash. My heart ached for my neighbour, who'd already gone out of her way to bring our kids home to safety when the evacuations started. I felt like we owed her so much more now that she'd won this morbid lottery.

"My house survived," I told Hitchcock.

"Fuckin' eh, man."

As we exited the wide glass doors, Heikel and Pellegrin caught up with us in the parking lot. They didn't want to be left behind. Can-TF2 and Incident Command wanted fair and equal opportunities for the now thousand firefighters in town, and were staging accordingly.

As I approached Steve Hansen, the captain still in charge of staging, to ask for a pump, Morari squabbled with him by Pumper 311, eager to get out there and keep working. The mouthy Saskatchewan girl in Morari was making a comeback. "Just let us go," she said. "There's no point in waiting for a call when the fire's still out of control."

"No, no," said Hansen, biting into a Subway sandwich. "No way, there's an order to things now."

Bread crumbs flaked off Hansen's lips as he laughed. "Motherfucker, where did you get that sandwich?" asked Morari.

"Damian," exclaimed Morari when she saw me limping along. "Holy shit, man. You're a legend!"

We all hugged and shook hands, trading stories before moving off with our respective crews. Hitchcock, Heikel, Pellegrin and I tracked down a colleague on his way to Fire Hall 5 in a fleet truck, and we climbed into the box.

Outside of hall 5, Can-TF2 was setting up trailers and generators side by side in the parking lot, as well as a cook shack. As we climbed out of the truck, what appeared to be a man in chef's whites waved at us. We limped in his direction, me still carrying my boots. "You guys look like you've worked hard," said the chef.

"Don't you know it," said Hitchcock.

"I'm cooking a spread. Should be ready in about twenty minutes."

Hitchcock shot off a group text to Jamieson, Relph and Shantz: *Best meal of your life at hall 5.* By the time they arrived, about thirty minutes later, the chef had prepared a feast. A slough of RCMP had also arrived and filled the bay where the buffet was about to begin. The firefighters, who wore soot on their faces like warrior paint and were dressed in disheveled uniforms, were told by the cook to go to the front of the line.

"Hey, now," said one cop, a barrel-chested gorilla of a man. "There's a lineup."

"Yes, and it starts behind us," said Jamieson.

"Just wait your turn," said the cop, to the agreement of the others, who were just as annoyed—and just as entitled—mumbling about how starved they all were.

"I don't think so," Relph interrupted.

"We haven't eaten in two days," Shantz said.

As the cook approached with the first tray of food, a voice in the back said, "The firefighters eat first." It was an RCMP sergeant. "They've been here for days with no food."

"Thank you," I said. "Look at them." I paused. "Just look. Look at their faces. They've been choking on smoke for forty-eight straight hours. Hardly a break, and nothing but snacks to keep them going. Let the boys eat. Besides, it looks like there's more than enough for everyone."

Radio chatter started picking up again, calling for help around the city. "Just about ready to go?" I asked Kyle. He nodded, stood and started cleaning his dish. "I'll get the other two."

Heikel and Pellegrin were sleeping on recliners in the TV room. I nudged Pellegrin, and they both woke up. "Radio's picking up. There's work to be done."

"Can we hold on just a few more hours?"

"Well, we're ready to go," I said. I gave them a second to make up their minds, but it was clear they'd hit their walls. "I'll see if others are ready. You keep resting. You were both a big help."

I returned to the kitchen, where Shantz, Relph and Jamieson devoured their food. "Who are you guys with?" I asked.

"Nobody," said Jamieson.

"Good. You guys are my crew now."

"Fuck yeah!" said Jamieson.

I pointed outside the window to a blue F-150. "That yours?" I asked Relph. He nodded. "You, Joe and Shantz take that. Me and Hitchcock will hop in my Tacoma. We're sticking together. If we get split up, do not go to Mac Island. You guys are with me now. We stay together. We fight together. We rest together. We're not getting separated."

"What about staging?" asked Shantz.

"This is our city," I said. "I know a lot of people have come to help, but this is still our city, and we will protect it." I turned to Hitchcock. "310's out back. It's got all our equipment on it. You can start there."

We plucked rakes, shovels, axes, piss-packs, garden hoses and whatever else our ad hoc crew could scavenge and load in our pickups. One of the boys snatched a Canadian flag from somewhere and brought it along. Hitchcock snapped a broomstick over his knee, pushed it through the side of the flag and zip-tied it to the grill of my Tacoma. All around us, guys were doing the same, and soon the sound of rattling flags cut through the ferocious wind.

Our first stop was Gregg Distributors, a massive grey building where I'd spent thousands of dollars over the course of my career as a contractor. Full as our trucks were with tools and resources, we needed more. We needed better. Not just for us, but for the rest of the Brotherhood. After acquiring permission from REOC, I earned the chance to do something I'd wanted to do my whole career.

I punched in a six-digit code on the keys of a Knox-Box, a little safe mounted outside the store and labelled "FD" for emergency personnel, and plucked the master keys from inside. The power was out. You couldn't see past the first twenty feet of each massive aisle. The boys pointed their flashlights, daunted by the thousands of shelves in the spotlight.

"We're gonna be here for hours," Shantz groaned.

Ring-ring.

They turned around, laughing louder than kids at a circus when I rolled by them on a push scooter shopping cart. "Okay," I said, tapping the steel basket mounted on the base, "what do we need?"

"Respirators," said Relph.

"Respirators, aisle sixteen. What else?"

"Clean coveralls," shouted Shantz.

"Coveralls, eighteen."

"Boots!"

"Gloves!"

"Boots, upstairs. Gloves are this way." I rang the bell twice. "Follow me."

"Jesus, Asher," said Relph, speed-walking behind me. "You own this place?"

We never took anything we didn't need, but we still managed to fill four shopping carts with goggles, shovels, gloves, headlamps, filters and every box of full-face, canister-style respirator masks we could find. Before this point, some had access to half masks, some to N95s that a house painter would barely tolerate, but the majority of us had no facial protection at all. Eyes watering and burning, you could hardly make out what was happening in front of you. Other guys had been stuck in their bunker gear since Tuesday morning, sweltering under the sun, the radiant heat and the thickness of inflammable Nomex. Great for house fires, terrible for wildfires. A lot of the crew would be desperate to swap them out for thinner coveralls.

We dropped half the load outside Mac Island, categorizing it in individual parking spaces. Firefighters in staging circled the gear like seagulls on scrap food, and the ground was bare in a heartbeat. Back in the Tacoma and F-150, we brought the other half load to dozens of personnel on the front lines.

"Everybody gets gloves," I called out to a Forestry crew cleaning up a brush fire. "Who wants respirators?" Hitchcock hollered to a pump in Prospect Pointe, still flowing water into basements to cool them. The response was elation and pure love as they caught what we tossed, and they repaid the favour with cigars (tobacco smoke inhalation, by this point, was inconsequential). It was an exchange not just of goods, but of stories and praise. We heard of how Steve Sackett entered his friend and colleague Trevor Mitchell's house to save Trevor's possessions, which he loaded into a baby bike trailer and pedalled to safety. How Randy Hoggarth drove his nine-months-pregnant wife, a firefighter herself, to Edmonton when the evacuations started, refilled his gas tank, and looped back to Fort McMurray to fight the fire. How firefighter Shawn Rommelaere had cut his Las Vegas vacation short and taken the first flight home when he heard about the fire on the news. In a way, the overstimulation, sleep deprivation and adrenaline rush he was getting on the ground in Fort McMurray was better than anything Sin City had to offer. And reuniting with the Brotherhood after two harrowing days was an even bigger high.

As we circled the city, making sure everyone had what they needed, we were also taking in the devastation of both the fire and the protective guard. On Tower Road, Acting Captain Cowan was working with a crew of probies, running hose, pumping out of the ponds and cleaning the hot spots, but the area looked like an entirely different region of the world. The forest was bulldozed one hundred fifty feet from the road, left in piles, as if they were preparing a new subdivision.

"Holy crap, Max, what the hell happened?" I asked.

"Welcome to the new Fort McMurray," he said. "Not quite the same again."

I stepped out of the driver's seat and handed over a bag of fresh coveralls. "Bet your boys could use these." We shook hands, and then he smiled like a boy on Christmas morning and pulled me in for a hug.

There was a mantra brewing from pump to pump—"Our city, our job!" They weren't about to hand the job off to someone else. When they got to Mac Island, they got the resources they needed and then got back to what they were doing before. There were no questions from the other departments' firefighters standing back in the queue; if this were their community, they'd be doing the same.

But it wasn't all fortitude and pride. Some guys griped about the jobs they had been assigned. Some were thought to be more glorified jobs, while others were seen as just work. But wherever we went, everyone we met, people thanked one another for what they were doing. Hearing people praise their crews so highly made me happier than ever that I'd decided to join the fire department instead of becoming an architect.

> The wind was fierce, and the morning's aerial reconnaissance put the size of the fire at eighty-five thousand hectares—bigger than Calgary.

It would have been too soon to call it a cause for celebration, though. The weather was cooler, but the wind was fierce, and the morning's aerial reconnaissance put the size of the fire at eighty-five thousand hectares—bigger than Calgary, Canada's second largest city by landmass. Abasand was again in the path of the flames, which were crawling west of the neighbourhood, while another fire stretched north from Saprae Creek and would only need one wind shift to point its flaming fingers at downtown. The Battle for Birchwood Trails was not over, either—downgraded, sure, but still on. As we dropped off respirator masks to Battalion Chief Woykin in Timberlea, he asked us to help douse spot fires in the forest south of the communities.

It was a lot of terrain for five us to cover in two vehicles, and some of the woodland areas were too narrow for the trucks. "Golf carts," said Jamieson. I was sure I misheard him, so I asked him to repeat it. "Golf carts."

Yup, he had sports on the mind again.

Relph explained that on Wednesday afternoon, as they were setting a sprinkler line in Wood Buffalo, reports came in of spot fires in the bush trails outside Thickwood. By then, Bugden's crew on Pumper 320 had grown to fourteen, so he could afford to lose a few. "We've got to send some guys there," Relph told him.

"Who do you want?" asked his captain. The three friends immediately volunteered, but they hadn't thought about how they'd get to the road seven kilometres away. Shantz, recalling his teenage years spent working at the golf course down the valley, wondered if the carts had been salvaged. They grabbed shovels, piss-packs and fire flappers—basically mud flaps on a stick—and, lucky for them, the carts had survived.

Remembering yet another old trick, Shantz hacked the carts to move faster by forcefully compressing governor springs in the motors with a key. As they cruised up the hill to Thickwood, Joe noticed Shantz looked concerned.

"What is it, buddy?" he asked.

"These are all GPS'd," he said. "If you get a certain distance away from the golf course, it cuts the power out." He turned behind him, realizing they were climbing a steep hill. "I think we're about to roll back down."

"Uhh, didn't the whole clubhouse burn to the ground?" asked Jamieson. "I think the GPS sensors are dead." He was right—they just kept going and going. They went from one edge of Thickwood to the other, hitting hot spots in trails too narrow for a fire truck to ever squeeze through.

It was a cute story, but I was skeptical. "We're not messing around here, guys," I said.

"Let's just go see if they're still there," Relph replied.

They were. I crossed over the scorched grass towards the carts, walked around their plastic shells and kicked at their thick eighteen-inch wheels. Turning back and forth between the gear in our truck and the carts, I had to admit it: "Yeah, these look useful."

Each man to a cart, we zoomed into the trails, bumping around the bush like back-road joyriders, braking and hopping to the scene of a hot spot. A flaming log? A smouldering grass patch? Find it. Fix it. Move on.

On Ermine Crescent, a Suncor pumper was having a bitch of a time trying to pour water on a brush fire. The hydrants were sucked dry, leaving them with limp hoses. As I zipped around, pumping the hand-nozzle attached to a piss-pack on hot spots around them, I noticed the leader of the pumper was Steve Morari. "Damian, Jesus Christ," he said, stunned. "I thought you were dead when I saw you sleeping earlier."

After a few hours, we dropped off the golf carts, hopped back in our personal vehicles and joined another operation. A disorganized pet rescue was in full effect, thanks to a Facebook page that had been created for evacuees who had to abandon their pets. They were posting their addresses by the dozens so firefighters in the area could help. Hitchcock's friend of a friend gave him her garage code, and he opened it. "I got it," I told him. "See if there are any more in the area."

Inside the kitchen sat two empty bowls on the floor. I filled one with water and checked the pantry for food. The rattling pellets summoned a scruffy little tabby from under a sofa. She seemed unfazed by the stranger in a red

> I called the family, just to hear the kids' voices again.

helmet, bravely trotting to me, nuzzling her head on my legs and circling me with a tail straight as an antenna. She seemed happier to see a human than the food itself. I picked her up and brought her to the bowl, and scratched under her chin as she chomped on it. After all the adrenaline pumping through my veins, after the high of reuniting with the Brotherhood, after the thrill of putting out spot fires that afternoon, the vibrations of her purring were a soothing remedy.

I called the family, just to hear the kids' voices again. Melanie gathered them in the camper with speakerphone on. They're normally such happy kids, talking over each other excitedly about their ordinary days, but it was hard to get a word out of them.

"When are you coming here?" asked Taya, practically whispering.

"I don't know."

"Are you safe?"

"I'm safe."

"When are we going home?" Aidan asked.

"We don't know yet. We won't know for a long time," I said. "Do you mind if your mom and me talk alone?"

Melanie turned off speakerphone, took her cell into a room and closed the door. "I'm trying to get confirmation on the house," she whispered. "Pam said it's okay, but there was a video from a helicopter on Facebook . . . I don't know, it didn't look good."

"I'll try to get out there," I told her, "but we're still doing our thing. It's busy."

"Paulette's dad said he was going out there with a camera," Melanie said, referring to a close neighbour. "She asked him to check up on our place. They say there are lots of spot fires still in Saprae. It could still go up."

I reassured her that the worst was probably over and said goodbye. It worried me, though, that Melanie seemed to know more than me. Had they sent enough personnel to Saprae? Were we so overloaded on the northwest side of town that they were letting the embers on the far east side of Wood Buffalo fall where they may? The fire was approaching downtown again, forcing crews to set up sprinklers on the east side of the lower townsite. The fire was on the north side across the Clearwater River. The river should have been enough to stop it, but the flames had jumped it once this week already, and if it happened again, there'd be a huge mobilization of forces in that small sector, and a lot of bodies to go around.

"Hey, Cap," said Relph behind me. "I was wondering if we could check out my house, or whatever's left of it."

"Of course," I said, giving the cat one last scratch before rising and walking to the Tacoma.

As I steered onto Abasand Drive, following Relph into the devastation, the uncertainty over my own home built inside of my stomach, filling me with anxiety. I had to keep it there. A good captain doesn't show his discomfort. A good captain is steady. But it was hard to ignore the repeated jolts to my guts every time the prognosis shifted from negative to positive to negative again. The tension swelled as I panned across a graveyard of former Abasand homes, their cement front steps scattered around the community like tombstones. Hitchcock and I hadn't seen it before that point. We'd only heard the battle over the radio, the endless attempts by the fire crews to get in and save what they could. It brought a tear to my eye seeing the devastation and thinking about what the crews must have gone through.

Relph parked by the corner of Aldergrove Avenue and Amberwood Crescent, and stepped into the ashes, leaving a thick footprint behind like he was trekking through Egypt's White Desert. Stripped of grass, you could see the property lines, where he had laid his sod and where his neighbour hadn't. That was pretty much all you could distinguish, except, ironically, for a perfect fire pit behind the ruin. The bricks and lid were intact, as if the flames were mindful not to inflict damage to their own kind.

Relph circumnavigated the house—not sobbing, not shaking, just flat—and plopped down on the front stoop, staring at his boots. I'm not sure what came over me, but I pointed my phone at him to capture this raw moment. He looked straight at me and let me take it.

"Can I see it?" asked Relph. I walked to him, holding out my phone. He took it from me and for a long quiet time stared at the screen, at himself, at his life, with a strange distance, as if it were an aged photo and not a rewind of thirty seconds ago. He shook his head with a slight grin. Then the phone pinged and the subtle amusement washed off his face. His eyes widened and his lips tightened. "I'm so sorry," he said, handing it back to me.

A notification of a text at the top of my screen wiped away just as I looked at the phone. I caught a flash of it, enough to feel the effect of the words before my brain had fully processed them.

Thu, May 5, 6:07 PM

Our house is gone. Confirmed.

CHAPTER 12

FORTITUDE

D riving northeast along Airport Road, flanked by charred trees and plumes in the sky, with Hitchcock quiet in the passenger seat, I thought about Melanie's rough transition to Fort McMurray and all the times I could see on her face that this wasn't quite the life she had imagined. She grew up in a tiny Saskatchewan town called Biggar, where her family still lived, and then moved to Vermilion, where we'd met, which was just a three-hour drive from them all. It had made weekend visits easy, but the five hours tacked to the road after she moved up here made home trips rare. The first few years in Fort McMurray felt isolating; she had no girlfriends and only knew my family and a few boys from the fire school she worked at. It wasn't until moving to Saprae, into our bungalow, that she had found a welcoming community and felt ready to set roots. Until then, she had thought Fort McMurray would be temporary. Turning onto Evergreen Place, to a freakishly random draw of standing homes and utter devastation, I wondered how she would feel if we lost the community we had come to love.

Among the ash, we covered the terrain like a rover on the moon. I pointed left and right, identifying the lost houses: "Marc and Kizzy's, gone. Frank and Barb's, gone. That's Pam and Manuel's. Gone." But after I parked at the edge of our driveway—now covered in the scraps of roof, wall and branches strewn across the neighbourhood—and saw the charred, broken bones of the walls I had framed, I had no words left in me. None. I just stared across the lot to a beige house two hundred metres behind it, unscathed and once unseen. With the fence of young poplars obliterated from view, my acreage had never looked so huge, and the task of building it from hand never seemed so grand. So grand, and yet so fragile.

Kyle squeezed my shoulder. I pulled the door handle and stepped out, sending a puff of ash streaming into the air. There was little I could recognize: the shell of our SUV, turned a charcoal colour, with empty spools for tires; my skidsteer, stripped to a rusty brown; a carpet of charred shingles from a swath of roof that had blown away and landed facedown, crumbled under my shoes; the blackened skeletons of my kids' bikes.

> There was little I could recognize: the shell of our SUV, turned a charcoal colour, with empty spools for tires.

I heard the slow patter of footsteps behind me as my crew followed me to the foundation. I stood at the edge, peering into the pit as it smoked like an inactive volcano. "I did everything I could," I said quietly. "I had the fire-resistant siding, the treated shingles." I trailed off, then walked the edges, narrating the ruin as if it were a floor plan again. "That's where my garage was. I kept my tools right there. That's the kitchen. Melanie thought the twenty-foot island was crazy, but we spent half our day there as a family. That's Taya's bike, gave it to her for her birthday in March. She hadn't even ridden it yet. That's where my guns were. A Winchester 30-30 Saddleside, like out of an old Western, something you pull off the side of your horse, crank and shoot. It was my dad's first gun—bought it when he was a kid and taught me to shoot with it. It's what I would have taught Aidan to hunt with when he was old enough." I sighed, wishing my dad had gotten a chance to see more than the blueprints before he died.

"And that over there . . . that's the safe where we kept the family photos." That one broke me. My lips quivered and tears slid down my cheeks. "It should be there. It was supposed to withstand up to eight hundred forty degrees for half an hour. It must have been so hot in here. So hot."

I trailed off, then walked the edges, narrating the ruin as if it were a floor plan again.

It was such a surreal sight that I think I had to say the words to process that it was real. I continued, "Those there were the kids' bedrooms. They slept in the same convertible beds I built them when they were babies. Took me sixty hours each. Solid oak and maple. No point in rebuilding them now. That room's mine and Melanie's. My nightstand . . ." I looked down to the basement, where an entire house had been turned into six inches of ash, and then to my naked left hand. "I kept my wedding ring in it."

I circled the whole pit, coming back to the old entrance, where shards of the white French doors mixed with rubble. "Hey, Damian," said Ralph, pointing his phone lens at me.

I took a few of my own pictures to send to Melanie, but first I sat alone in the truck and called her. I couldn't say much else but "sorry." My hands were shaking as I held back tears. "We'll get through it. I promise you," I mustered. "We are going to get through it." Melanie was silent, stronger than me in that moment. At least now the family had closure, because knowing everything was gone was somehow easier than not knowing for sure. She spent the entire night and next day alone in the trailer, shutting herself out from the other McMurrayites camped at the grounds. Melanie doesn't let people see her pain.

Hitchcock opened the driver's side door and put a hand on my shoulder. "I'm sorry, Cap," he said. "You want me to drive?"

"Negative," I replied. We had to prepare for the next task, and it wasn't long before we saw it.

As we crossed the highway heading back into town, we spotted a fresh plume rising in the bushes south of the road. I radioed for help. "Command from Captain Asher," I said.

"Go for command," said dispatch.

"Located one kilometre east on Airport Road. We have a forest fire sparking up. Requesting two tankers and a pump truck."

"Okay, working on it. Stay in your location."

By my estimation it was fifty feet wide and three hundred feet deep into the bush.

Along with the tankers and an FMFD squad truck, a Calgary pump and ladder arrived. They jumped out of the trucks and started laying hose lines, while my guys geared up in masks, balaclavas and gloves, ready to get deep into the forest as the trees candled and the fire blew a blinding smoke towards us.

"Where are your piss-packs?" I asked.

"They don't work," the Calgary captain said. "We need a water bomber."

Maybe working in the boreal for fifteen years had spoiled me. Or maybe they were the spoiled ones. "Show me what you've got," I said.

A Calgary firefighter climbed to the top of the truck, tossing piss-packs from out of the top cubby to the boys. "They don't do shit," he said as he threw the first one to Relph. "They're leaking," he said, throwing the second to Jamieson. "They're empty and we can't even fill 'em," he said, giving the last two to Hitchcock and Shantz.

I looked at the gear. They were beautiful plastic tanks, not the flimsy rubber bags we were used to, and bright yellow without a mark on them. The only reason they leaked was because the O-rings weren't screwed on right. My boys tightened the fittings, straightened the O-rings, pulled them onto their backs and were ready to get into the fight.

A tanker operator filled their packs, and then they sprinted into the flames and smoke to attack the front of the fire, making a wet line around the perimeter. They ran back to the truck, grabbed axes, refilled the piss-packs and scrambled back to the fire to hack down trees, extinguish them on the ground and stomp and grind little embers jumping at their shoes. Their coveralls were soaked to the knees, their feet were burning, but there wasn't a whimper as they assaulted the flames. I stood in the ditch with the other captain, arms crossed, admiring their work.

"You guys are nuts," he said.

"You guys are nuts,"
he said.
"We do it often.
It's just what we're
used to."

"We do it often. It's just what we're used to."

The firefighters cooled the area from the edge of the bush, trying to keep the flames from pushing into unburned forest. After the third round, my crew was ready to take the nozzle out of their hands and into the bush, but by the time they climbed out of the ditch, the Calgary crew was re-racking the hose.

"Listen," said their captain, "we've got strict rules: we're only allowed to advance fifty feet into the trees."

"How are you guys making out?" I asked my guys.

"We've almost got the front edge," said Hitchcock. "The fire will hold."

"Can you stay longer?" I asked the captain.

"Sorry," he replied. "We'll get our piss-packs back from you later."

I thanked him and called Incident Command for air support. "We'll try," I was told.

As the Calgary crew packed up, the wind changed direction, just about blowing the advancing fire out. We waited until the water bombers arrived and finished the job.

"All right," I said, "let's get some breakfast. I'm famished." They all looked at their watches with concerned looks. "What's wrong?"

"It's, uhh," started Shantz, "it's like eight at night."

"Well, then," I said, "let's get some dinner."

We were all bagged, we all looked a mess, and I could feel myself getting loopy. On the road to town, I must have asked Hitchcock how his condo was doing three times, seven minutes apart, each time forgetting he'd already said it was fine. When he'd ask me questions, my answers were delayed, and I couldn't remember what question I was answering half the time. We arrived at Fire Hall 3 late at night, to refuel on grub and let the boys sleep, but I wasn't ready to shut my eyes.

The fire on the west and north sides of town had spread to a few homes and structures in north Abasand. Crews were patrolling Timberlea, making sure embers didn't get out of hand. Ground crews were still soaking spot fires in Birchwood Trails and Tower Road. Another massive set-up was protecting the airport, which was once again under threat. And dozens of trucks from across Alberta were setting up in downtown, ready to roll. On the northeast side of the Athabasca River, winds had shifted towards town, and the Beast was ready for another main-event bout. This time it was coming for the heart of our city, hoping to tear it up with every major business and amenity that was vital to supporting our community.

A fleet of heavy equipment readied for the encore, but they'd have to fight without aerial support—it was too dark for choppers and tankers, so we did the best we could. There were a thousand bodies scattered across downtown, bracing for a Herculean scrap. But as they readied for the showdown, the oil plants went under high alert and had to call back their trucks and firefighters, leaving us short a few dozen men and without their incredible apparatus. It was hard, too, to stomach the fact that these guys had sacrificed so much to help our community and we couldn't reciprocate.

My crew and I didn't have a fire truck, so we had to helplessly watch everything unfold from hall 3's parking lot, perched on a hill in Thickwood with a great vantage point of the lower townsite. We sat patiently waiting for the call telling us where we could assist—which truck, which unit would require extra manpower. The distant red glow in front of me rose to an ominous size. The fire was approaching us from the north side of the Athabasca and Clearwater Rivers, crawling down the riverbank like lava oozing from a volcano. By now, we knew damn well that it could jump the river—just as it had a few days ago, when everything was set in motion—and redeploy its army of embers into Birchwood Trails through the park's east side. The radio started picking up noise from pumpers taking their positions.

> The fire was approaching us from the north side of the Athabasca and Clearwater Rivers, crawling down the riverbank like lava oozing from a volcano.

We waited for deployment in hall 3, where Sarah Vincent, a paramedic with the FMFD, was looking after crews all week. She managed to procure loads of food from an industrial camp her mom worked at, and she offered me some microwaved lasagna.

"Geez, Captain," she said, handing me the plastic container, "you look a little dirty. Would you like some laundry done? I've got some spare clothes you can take for an hour."

Looking at my uniform, I could hardly tell it had once been blue. "I would love that," I said.

After the hot meal, I changed into a pair of shorts and a T-shirt, handed Sarah my grimy uniform and lay down on a couch, where I fell asleep to the radio. There were fire trucks from just about every department in Alberta staged on every street downtown, bracing for the worst. I dozed off, imagining the once unimaginable loss.

I wasn't asleep for long. As the number of trucks and resources outgrew Mac Island, hall 3 was being set up as a second staging point, and the arriving captains started kicking out the crews that weren't officially deployed there. When Hitchcock and the boys came to get me, someone tried to stop them. "No, leave Damian here. He needs his sleep."

"Negative," said Relph. "He's coming with us. Where we go,

Cap goes. Captain's orders." He rustled me awake and helped me to my feet. I was woozy, slurring in a voice cracked from shouting orders for three days. "Wass happening? Wherrrre we going?"

"My house," said Shantz, pulling my arm over his neck. "Everything's still happening downtown, but we gotta go." Hitchcock took my other arm as we hobbled outside to the Tacoma. There were a few other crews and free agents funnelling out with us, banished from the hall. "Nay-thannn," I said—or, at least, tried to say—when I spotted Nathan Cseke climbing into his truck. Knowing downtown was under threat, I told him, "Don't go to staging."

"No worries," he said. "I'm sleeping in my bed tonight."

I nodded, fishing for my keys in slow motion. "You want me to drive?" Hitchcock asked apprehensively.

It took me five seconds to process his question. "No," I slurred. "It's good. I'm good. I got this." The boys stared at each other with bulging eyes.

"Oh-kay," he managed to force out of his skeleton smile.

Lucky for Hitchcock, it was a short drive—one I'll never remember. But I have a blurry memory of the boys helping me inside, practically carrying me up the stairs, helping undress me and tucking me into bed. I was drained, but a terrible feeling was banging from my subconscious. "Where's Cseke?" I asked (or so I'm told).

"He's at home," said Shantz. "Sleeping."

"He can't stay there alone," I said, somehow remembering that Nathan lived in Dickinsfield, on a tree line of Birchwood Trails that joined the Athabasca River valley. If the fire could jump to downtown, then it could jump to the trails, too. If he was as bagged as me, then there'd be no one to shake him awake if his house caught fire. "Gimme my phone," I said. Trevor fished it from the pocket of my pants on the floor. Somehow I was lucid enough to unlock it and find Cseke in my contacts.

"Sssekky. Sssekky."

"Damian?" he asked, no doubt bewildered.

"You've got to get out of your house. Right. Now."

"Why?"

"I'm hearing reports that the fire is about to jump the river. It could hit Birchwood Trails, so you can't be home alone. You've got to get out. Get over here."

"Where?"

I must have looked around the room for a long hard moment. "I don't have a fucking clue." That was the last thing I said and I gave the phone to Shantz.

"Nathan, it's Trevor."

"What is he talking about?"

"I think he's saying you're not safe. You need to get over here. I'll give you the address."

Thankfully, as our heads dropped, so did the temperature, suffocating the Beast and squeezing the life from it just as it neared the river. The raging wall of fire slowed and fizzled to a manageable blaze, a standard wildfire that we'd all seen before, with spot fires igniting ever so slowly and extinguishing quickly as firefighters stamped them out with their shovels. As the men and women on the ground got ahead of the flames, the fire became an almost calm and peaceful sight. The Beast, as the world now knew it, had come in like a lion, but it went out like a mouse.

The room I woke up in four hours later was a mystery to me. My duffel bag was on the floor, and I could see my truck out the window. I grabbed a folded towel on the foot of my bed, stepped into the en suite shower and stared down at my mangled feet as greyish brown water swirled around them. It was freezing, but a cold shower is still a shower. And though I didn't look any cleaner after—and no doubt ruined Shantz's towels for good—I felt fresher than I had in a long time. I unfolded the clean uniform Sarah had washed for me, buttoned my shirt and fastened my belt into my FMFD buckle.

Downstairs, Hitchcock, Relph, Jamieson and, for some reason, Nathan Cseke were passed out on sofas. The walls were decorated with Oilers memorabilia, and on TV Don Cherry was giving the Fort McMurray Fire Department a huge shout-out on Coach's Corner. No matter my opinion on men's organized figure skating, it was a great feeling. It was the first time I remembered there was still a world outside of Wood Buffalo. It was inspiring to see the rest of Canada and beyond stepping up to support our community, one whose true face the country was seeing for the first time.

I scooped coffee grounds into the machine, filled the carafe, turned it on and took my first fresh cup in days onto the back deck, enjoying the peaceful quiet in the city. Despite the poor visibility, Fort McMurray had that enjoyable natural wood campfire odour I love. Sitting in a deck chair, reminiscing about the last three days, I wondered how long I would be able to enjoy the moment. Would the temperature heat back up again, sending us into another major attack? Or could we start breathing a little easier?

I finished my coffee and returned to the kitchen, where Relph was filling up a mug for himself. I knew how much the guy loves to eat— he practically makes a hobby out of it.

"Thinking of making the boys breakfast," I said. "Want to give me a hand?"

"I'll drive," he said, dropping the coffee back in the pot.

We left the house and made our way to the Sobeys a short drive away. There wasn't much left in the coolers and on the shelves, but I cleaned out what I could: thawed bacon and sausage, days-old bread and pancake batter, maple syrup, eggs and bags of soggy hash browns. I snatched a sack of pet food off the shelves too, and stopped at Hitchcock's friend's place to pay her cat a visit.

Back at the house, the sweet, fatty scent of bacon wafted through the living room and bedrooms, waking the boys. "Whoa, what the hell is this?!" said Jamieson when his eyes caught sight of the grand slam breakfast I was prepping.

"Jesus, Cap," exclaimed Shantz. "You need a hand?"

"Just about done," I said, flipping a pancake. A loud meow from the corner of the kitchen caught their attention. Their heads tilted sideways, confused by the scruffy tabby crunching on her pellets in a bowl on Shantz's floor. "She's with me."

> We set the plates and food together and had our table talk for the day, promising again to stick together for as long as it would take to finish the fight—and we knew it would take weeks.

We set the plates and food together and had our table talk for the day, promising again to stick together for as long as it would take to finish the fight—and we knew it would take weeks.

"You know," Shantz said, looking at his brother-in-law with a mouth full of toast, "this has been the best and worst time of my life."

Relph's eyes closed and his grin widened. "This has only been the best."

CHAPTER 13

REBUILD

A strip of wet sandpaper scraped my stubbly neck. My eyes opened, looking into the deep green eyes of the tabby on my chest, lapping my face. I lay there awhile, under a floral wallpaper, until my alarm clock went off and it was time to work.

It was the morning of Monday, May 9, seven days since the battle began, and I'd been staying in a hotel north of town with the rest of the Fort McMurray Fire Department. Up until that point, we had been working out of the halls, making our own shifts and prioritizing the work that was left. The fire was past us, but there was still plenty to do. Finally, the day before, on Sunday, management had said they were going to move into a rotation and put us in hotel rooms, where at least there were working gas lines and meals for us. Rotation would be three days, three nights, and it would start with A-shift—my shift—the next day. I saw despair in my brothers and sisters, upset they'd have to do another six days straight. We were on the verge of an uprising. Management then briefed us that due to the length of time we'd already put in, they'd rotated shifts around and A-shift would do a single day shift and three nights, instead of rolling right into six. Battalion Chief Mike Woykin made some changes to the roster too, putting me in charge of Joe, Kyle, Relph and Trevor.

By that Monday, the fire had grown to over two hundred

thousand hectares and was spreading to the Saskatchewan border, but the city limits were safe. Alberta Premier Rachel Notley and dozens of journalists arrived to survey the aftermath that morning, but back at the halls, it was business as usual. Sort of—there was a hell of a lot of cleaning to do. Most of the halls had been dump zones for supplies. Despite the mess, a swell of pride hit us like a hurricane as soon as our shoes touched the bay's red floor at hall 1. We were limited on our supplies, working with burned hose, lost chainsaws and broken axes. We did an inventory of what was working, what wasn't and what needed replacing. Mechanics had worked around the clock to repair rescue trucks, pumpers, medics and Brontos that had seen more action in one week than most apparatus would in an entire life cycle. The trucks were caked with ash, the concrete floor with mud, and muddy hand lines criss-crossed everywhere. Inside the kitchen, stacks of dirty dishes smelled rancid.

It was disgusting, but I didn't have to say anything to my crew. Every firefighter and paramedic had already taken a job—mopping floors, scrubbing trucks, storing equipment.

I grabbed a hose and washed a pumper. The military pride in our work and presentation overcame us, and the old regiment mentality washed over the fire hall. After cleaning, I turned my attention to the mountain of food that had been dropped in the kitchen. There was a kitchen at Mac Island at this point, and that was the plan for lunch, but there was nothing wrong with the food we had on hand. I started sorting and cooking at the same time, and before long, the crews were drawn from the bays by the smell of lunch. We sat in our kitchen and had a traditional lunch as a shift—something that we had not had in weeks—telling stories and reminiscing about the past few days.

That night, I decided I'd spend the night somewhere else. After work, I dropped Hitchcock off at the hotel and fed the cat. The

Alberta Fire Fighters Association had set up an open-door shopping spree, donated by Mark's Work Warehouse, for any firefighter who'd lost their home to take whatever they needed from the clothing store. As much as I wanted to see my family, all I owned was my stinking uniform. I grabbed three pairs of jeans, a couple of pairs of shorts, some shirts, a jacket, and a pair of shoes—now the only non-work clothes to my name. I didn't bother putting them on yet, though; seeing the family was more important.

It was 10:30 p.m. when I pulled into the campground and bee-lined straight for our RV, past the other evacuees calling for me.

"Damian!"

"Captain!"

"Can we talk for a minute?"

"Is it safe to go back?"

I waved at them and quickened my pace. I walked up the steps to our brown camper and knocked on the door. Melanie looked confused when she answered, as though she didn't recognize me or comprehend why I was there. Then she clamped my cheeks between her palms and kissed me before bursting into tears. We embraced tightly, for a long minute.

"Daddy!"

I turned around to see Taya, Aidan and Petzl running through the RV lots in shorts and tees. They pounced up the camper steps and wrapped their arms around my legs. I crouched down and kissed them, while the dog hopped around us, wagging her brown tail.

Aidan looked up at me with big eyes and asked ever so quietly, "Are you finished fighting the fire?"

"Not until tomorrow," I said, tussling his hair. "But I'm here tonight."

This was how shifts always used to start and finish, with seeing my family, so the night almost felt normal. We spent it as a unit, telling them stories about the incredible battle—saving people from trapped vehicles, bulldozing houses, riding around in golf carts to keep the fire from growing. My kids always looked up to firefighters, naturally, but in that moment they looked at me as if I were a superhuman.

I tucked them into the same bed. Cleaned up, shaved and climbed into the double bed with Melanie. I held her tightly as she lay her head on my bare body. "What is it?" I asked.

"You smell like smoke." She would tell me this for the next two months. My skin had absorbed so much smoke, you'd think I had just been sitting beside a campfire for a week straight.

The next morning, I stayed in uniform and met with displaced McMurrayites staying at the RV park, reassuring them that the fire was under control and the worst was behind them. Most people's biggest concern was not knowing whether their house was gone or still standing. As firefighters, we always want to help, so I asked each person to list their name, address and phone number, and I would try my best to gather information for them all when I returned to work for my night shift.

After I got back to Fort McMurray, in between work and delivering updates to my friends and neighbours, I spent every other daylight hour in Saprae Creek, digging through an entire life's contents of ash, shovelling piles of it into a barrel, panning it like a gold miner, dumping and repeating.

There wasn't much there. Melanie's jewellery had melted into tiny abstract sculptures, and my grandfather's Rolex was worth less than a candy necklace. I found the Winchester my dad gave me, warped and twisted, with the stock burned off; I plan to turn it into a plaque one day. Two kiln-dried vases that Melanie made in a pottery class a decade ago were intact; less so the porcelain casts of our babies' hands and feet, just three white fingers and a chip of a heel. Not sure whose was whose, I salvaged what I could and kept digging, with one important thing in mind.

On Sunday, May 15, the thirteenth straight day of fighting the Horse River Fire, everyone in the department was given six days off. It was a bittersweet goodbye at the hotel that morning. As the caravan of vehicles moved along Highway 63 as one, before splitting off at our respective exits—to Saskatchewan, to B.C., to Edmonton International Airport—we passed each other with a wave. The feeling was the end of an era, that things would truly never be the same again when we returned.

I found the Winchester my dad gave me, warped and twisted, with the stock burned off; I plan to turn it into a plaque one day.

Three members of the department, including Randy Hoggarth, had had babies during the fire and likely saw their newborns for the first time since delivery. Kyle Hitchcock flew back to Ontario to see his family, and while he was in Mississauga, he met up with Joe Jamieson to see the Toronto Raptors thump the Miami Heat in a Game 7 playoff match. The week in hell only cemented their decisions to make careers as firefighters in northern Alberta.

Tia and Steve Morari tried to take a break at a picturesque family lake lot on Regina Beach, but someone had other plans for them. A puffy brown plume in the bush caught their attention, and by then they'd seen enough of those to know it was more than a campfire. In their beach clothes, they told the neighbours of the blazing house to wet their properties, then started pulling hose with the volunteer fire department. They became folk legends as word spread through the small community of the Fort McMurray firefighters who'd come to the rescue.

Trevor Shantz and Chris Relph became closer brothers during the fire, and drove together in Shantz's truck to see their families in Edmonton. It seemed to Relph that his newborn daughter had grown so much in those two weeks, she had become more interactive. It also seemed to him she'd forgotten who he was, but just as quickly as she had lost recognition of him, she grew fond of her daddy and the carriage strolls they took around Edmonton.

Captain Ryan Pitchers was also in Edmonton, at the bedside of his ailing father, who'd been battling stage 4 lung cancer for a year— and somehow winning. On those quiet nights, he found himself wondering why his home in Wood Buffalo Estates was spared when so many others, including those of department members, burned to the ground. *Could we have done more? Could we have been stronger? Why did they lose everything, and not me?* As firefighters, we're all self-critical, but officers more than others. It's a leadership instinct to go back in your mind and replay scenarios, ponder what you could have done differently, but that good quality can haunt you, too.

I spent my six days at the camper.

"I've got something for you," I told Melanie shortly after arriving. "Put out your hand." I gently placed it in her palm. She gasped.

"No way," she exclaimed, bringing my wedding band to her eye for inspection. It was a little dinged up around the edges, but otherwise just as I'd left it in the nightstand before my shift started.

I spent the rest of my days off busily making sure the family was comfortable. I upgraded our weekend camper to a two-bedroom unit that could last for a couple of years, set up the sewer lines and worked tirelessly to make sure Melanie had everything she needed so her hands were free.

In my brief breaks, I sat at a picnic table with a cold cider, amazed at how fast things had changed from the weeks before. At times, I worried about the rest of my firefighting career while I grappled with respiratory problems. Even under perfect air quality, I was short on breath and wheezy. Kicking a soccer ball around the lake with Aidan for two minutes would bring me to my knees.

By the time we returned from our break, management had issued us all full wild land masks, the T-1000 canister style we'd only had in short supply during the fight. Most of us had inhaled or absorbed transdermally an unprecedented volume of natural woodland smoke and noxious hydrocarbons from burning houses. It's not as bad as New York's first responders, who inhaled cancerous amounts of concrete particles, had to face, but it's safe to say the Horse River Fire will take years off some of our lives.

The doctors prescribed me an inhaler and steroids for my lungs. I noticed the vast majority of the guys carrying similar medicine around the hall, but nobody talked about it. There was an unspoken rule about it. That, and using the "H-word." Nobody dared call themselves a hero, even if everyone outside the department was saying it. That's not what we were. We were simply the people who did their job when they were called upon. Anytime we were out of town, at a cafe or restaurant, staff took one look at our FMFD hats and the meal was free. It was appreciated, of course, but we were quick to remind them we were just doing our jobs.

Besides, the real test was going to be how folks would react once they saw Fort McMurray with their own eyes. The frustrations of locals mounted as the date for reentry remained a mystery, and among the firefighters there was a lot of uncertainty about whether the public would accept our best efforts when they returned, or whether they'd return at all. Even before the fires, a good number of McMurrayites had been laid off or were on the edge of foreclosure as home values collapsed. Would they see this as their ticket out?

Until then, the city remained a zombie-land. Downtown, the stench of rotting restaurant food and butcher meat mixed with the lingering campfire smell. As we patrolled the city, looking for hot spots and wood piles that could re-ignite, we'd stop and reflect at the scene of streets filled with abandoned cars and houses with their bedroom lights still on. I'd wait to see someone move inside, but it was hollow. No children played in the parks. No planes flew overhead. The city belonged to wild game roaming in from their devastated habitats.

The final toll was over 1,500 structures destroyed, including at least 2,500 residences. In all, more than half of Abasand Heights and three-quarters of Beacon Hill were wiped out. A third of Saprae Creek and a good chunk of Wood Buffalo had vanished, as well as a large chunk of Stonecreek. And all the heritage that had once endured in Waterways, our oldest neighbourhood, would have to live on through archival records. An official government assessment said 15 percent of Fort McMurray was gone. I thought a better way to look at it was that 85 percent of Fort McMurray was saved. But there was no guarantee that McMurrayites, when they returned—if they returned—would see it the same way.

Before the sun rose on Thursday, June 2, we unloaded two park benches from a squad truck onto the King Street Bridge and sat between two ladder trucks with their sticks pointed diagonally forwards, holding a massive Canadian flag on a rope over Highway 63. At any moment, locals would be driving below.

I anxiously waited with a dozen firefighters from two crews, sitting on bumpers, atop the truck or leaning against the rail, ready to welcome them back. Some of us were skeptical of this homecoming photo-op at first—the fire had grown to 550,000 hectares, and though it was mostly in the hands of forestry workers and specially hired firemen from as far away as South Africa, lots of work was still needed to repair tools and apparatus. Parts of the trucks on the bridge were held together with duct tape and haywire, and one of the trucks had a smashed window. We didn't look much better in our ripped and torn uniforms. I was feeling a bit on edge, like a playwright after opening night nervously awaiting the morning's reviews.

Knots in my stomach untangled as cars approached, honking louder than a flock of geese. At first they trickled, but as the day grew brighter it was a gridlock again, but without the panic. As we peered into the windshields of cars below, locals smiled and waved back at us. It was a sweet and badly needed medicine.

Soon people were out of their cars, walking along the bridge with food, coffee and donuts. Sometimes, I sensed they'd prepared a speech in their heads, but more often than not those scripts were abandoned. Eyes welled, voices cracked, and all they could do in the end was give us a handshake or a hug. It was much more than words could ever say.

Firefighters don't ask for help or a thank-you, so for people to go out of their way to show their appreciation, however they could muster it, was a phenomenal feeling. The bridge welcoming became almost a 24/7 operation. For the next three days, guys sat on the bumper until three in the morning some nights, exchanging war stories and waving at every passing car. We didn't want to miss a single one.

Of course, not everyone was impressed with us. Some could only see what they'd lost and ignored the bigger picture. How do you even begin to convince a homeowner that destroying all their assets to save another's is part of the greater good? A few folks walked to the bridge just to say we should have fought harder, that we should have saved their house. RCMP and other personnel who came to our defence would point out that members on the bridge had lost their houses, too, but had still remained to fight.

Everywhere you looked, a sea of bumper stickers and signs

proclaimed We Will Rebuild or Fort Mac Strong, but people were in a variety of mind states, depending on whether their homes were gone, damaged or still standing, depending on whether they were well insured, underinsured or not insured at all, or just depending on the type of person they were on any given day. If there's one thing I've learned about human beings as a first responder, it's that you can grapple with grief in two ways: carry it gracefully, embrace the tests of strength and the growth inside of you, or wade into your anger and bitterness. Often it's a roller coaster of both.

The worst was the pain we felt at Emily Ryan's funeral. We all respected her father, Cranley, a training officer who lost two members of his family during the fire. Members of the volunteer crews from Anzac, Fort McKay and Saprae Creek, along with industrial firefighters from Syncrude, Suncor and CNRL, were there, too. It was the first time since the battle started that we'd met up with them. Everybody was taking the loss hard. Fire departments are like families, and when a member loses a loved one, it feels like a loss of our own. Cranley's tragedy could have happened to any one of us.

Access to Saprae Creek Estates started the next day, but we didn't want the kids to see it yet, so they stayed behind with friends at the campground. Waiting for Melanie at the edge of our driveway, now a little road to nowhere, I wondered if she was psychologically prepared to see the wreckage. I'd sent her dozens of photos in the meantime, but disasters often don't sink in until you've seen them with your own eyes.

Not Melanie, though. She was strong-headed, stepping out of the SUV and trudging through the ash with a stoic face. Anything recognizable was literally a shell of its former self, but the only thing that shocked her was the massive landscape. Before the fire, she couldn't see the next house from our bedroom windows; now she could see all the way to the ski hill two kilometres away, and what remained of our community in between. There was no rhyme or reason to the destruction. A cul-de-sac would be completely intact but for one unlucky home, or completely obliterated but for a random survivor. From a bird's-eye view, it would have resembled a chessboard with no strategy.

Walking through Saprae holding hands, we saw friends returning to their properties, many as unlucky as us. Afterwards, Melanie's girlfriends had a little gathering at one of the better houses, and by the time she left, the reason why we'd come back wasn't even a question anymore. She remembered why Saprae was home, and it had little to do with the house or landscape.

Not everyone returned, though. As months past, as wreckage was cleared and scorched lawns were torn up and tilled, I saw more For Sale signs than in the 1990s. Businesses didn't reopen, apartment vacancies spiked, and some of Aidan and Taya's schoolmates weren't back in September. Some schools had to merge because of low enrolment. A small portion of the city had given up on Fort McMurray.

We felt the shrinkage at work. Call volumes dropped, and all those promises from the last two years—extra manning, new equipment, updated trucks, Fire Halls 6 and 7—all of it was even farther away, as the municipality focused on rebuilding. At $3.58 billion, it was the biggest insurance

> It's like being an athlete, wondering if you should retire at your peak or wait for bad knees to set in.

loss in Canadian history, and it took a huge toll, causing even more layoffs, more hurt, more anger. Firefighting training was suspended until 2017, forcing probies like Matthew Heikel and Christine Pellegrin, who had done more hours in a week than most firefighters do in fifteen, to wait a long time for their Level 1 certificates. On those quieter nights in the hall, with little to do, I contemplated my future as a firefighter, or whether I wanted that future at all. An event of that magnitude throws everything into question. It's like being an athlete, wondering if you should retire at your peak or wait for bad knees to set in.

That November, the department was hit with more bad news. Our brother, Bo Cooper, firefighter 395, lost his battle with leukemia. More members stepped up for the planning of his funeral than I'd ever seen before, and tens of thousands of citizens came out for his parade on Franklin Avenue. It was a powerful ceremony for someone who'd touched about every life in the department during the battle, rallying us online. A number of firefighters from departments that had come to assist us in May were there for the funeral, and we finally had a chance to thank them.

The community spirit started picking up again around Christmastime with physical evidence of the rebuild impossible to ignore. Call volumes picked up again as people started moving back into the city in larger numbers, and soon the FMFD started hiring again. Four hundred houses had grown from the ashes, and the excavating, framing and siding of the next fifteen hundred was happening at a staggering speed. Ninety houses in Prospect had already been started, and every day in Wood Buffalo there was a new house finished, or a new business opened. Not all the stores were what they were before, and many of the homeowners were new to the city, but the attitude behind Fort Mac Strong and We Will Rebuild was becoming truer as things returned to something like normal.

It'll never be the same again, of course, but in some ways the feeling in the community is better than before. During the boom, Fort McMurray had become a revolving door of opportunists, dreamers, boot-strapped workhorses and the upwardly mobile, who rarely took the opportunity to know their neighbours. But in the weeks after the fire, the people were as friendly as I remembered them in my childhood, even more so. It was not unusual for customers to hug my mom at the grocery store. Not because she had lost anything—she hadn't—but because they'd experienced a traumatic event together, and were getting through it together.

Perspectives change. Priorities shift. Fort McMurray had been so lucrative that people practically set their money on fire. It was nothing for guys, the day before a hunting trip, to drop $15,000 on a new ATV, and then sell it for half the price on Craigslist six months later. No doubt, even my son was upset to learn his quad had been destroyed. But he was also happier than ever to have his lucky blanket. Taya gripped her hippo tighter than ever. Losing almost everything makes you appreciate every other small thing.

I could only predict the hardships ahead. Winter would be coming, and there was so much work required to reestablish my family. But when I look back on the fire, I see another family formed within the Fort McMurray Fire Department. I see boys who've accepted other boys as brothers. Girls who've accepted other members as siblings. Captains who look to their firefighters as their sons and daughters. And they know the officers they can trust, who'll never let them down. We've seen the limits of what people will do, the sacrifices they're willing to make, and I know without a doubt that the guys on the floor would follow me to the end and never turn their backs on me.

The Horse River Fire gave the world a vivid image of what Fort McMurray is really about. What it's made of. Why we call it home.

EPILOGUE

I jump on the concrete frame of my home in one hop, edge-walk towards the middle of the foundation and then climb down a ladder to fix a lopsided wood beam dangling from a crane above. It's March in Saprae Creek; I can't feel my fingertips as I tighten the pulley rope around the beam, but I can see my breath inside the four-thousand-square-foot pit. The concrete is a few months old and the concrete footings below the ladder are brand new, holding vertical low-bearing loads inside. I shimmy the rope to the centre of the horizontal beam until it's more or less balanced, ascend the ladder and walk carefully to the edge of the eight-inch-thick wall.

This is how I've spent the majority of my days since the fall, in my second uniform: a raggedy hoodie, grey pants, muddy sneakers and a ball cap with a visor so bent that I work halfway in tunnel vision. It helps me focus. Six months into construction and there's at least sixteen more to go. But I've already finished the exterior of the shop, fourteen hundred square feet on each storey, and heated it for the family to occupy while I rebuild outside. Since January, we've lived partially in the furnished four-bay garage and partially in the camper parked inside of it. Before that, we stayed with Jonathan and Kelly, truly the best neighbours anyone could ask for. What I did to deserve such patient friends and family, I'll never know.

I jump off the edge and land in a frozen tire track with a thud. We had an early and heavy dump of snow this season, which is to say we've had a normal northern winter. By the time it all melts, the ground will be good and moist to protect us in fire season. I step around a bundle of windowpanes, a utility hose and a pile of flattened boxes, for a heater and a staple gun—all new, of course—and step into a zoom boom. I pull the crane toggle, lifting the beam halfway across the foundation and delicately steering it between the middle and end loads. Once it's in place, I get out, hop atop the wall again and walk to the edge of the beam. It's at least six inches too long to fit inside the slots. I need to take a chainsaw to it.

Ten steps from the garage, I stop. *Right. There is no chainsaw.* I unlock my phone and add it to a note:

Things to Buy

Kids' boots
Snowboard helmets
Generator
Booster cables
Ballpoint pens
Chainsaw

There are, however, a few other silver linings to starting over from scratch. For one, we're a lot more selective with our purchases and better at living without wants (snowboarding not included). There were features in the old house that we said we'd do differently again—and now we have to. We also decided against rebuilding the rental, which let us change the orientation of the house for a future swimming pool without any risk of trees falling into it. Our two-acre perimeter is barren now. The tallest timber is wood stakes tied with flapping pink tape to delineate our property line. It'll be seven years before the young poplars I'm planting are high enough to re-create that beautiful, woodsy fortress. As for the rest of the Fort McMurray landscape, my kids will be in a seniors' home before it resembles the one of their early childhood.

Along with this community's reputation and the people themselves, the topography has drastically changed. On hikes through the Wood Buffalo neighbourhood, you get a whole new perspective, not just seeing more of the rivers and creeks, but hearing them better too. You'll notice the randomness of the blaze, in the strips of clearances, opening like mysterious back roads, and the success of the firefighters when the scorched woods abruptly become a wall of lush green. But even some of the surviving trees needed clearing. The fire weakened their trunks until they keeled over at the shove of wind, or probably would if they weren't chopped down first. The Birchwood Trails system has been cleared of all the potential fallers, as well as an extra hundred feet of fine timber that once backed up on houses. Entering a greenbelt directly from your backyard walkout used to be something realtors bragged about. Now it's a liability.

Shuffling over tundra on my property, crushing charred pinecones under my feet, I can feel on my cheeks how thinned-out the region is. With so much of our fortress removed, the wind barriers broken, living in the north is even colder. I blow warm air into my cupped hands and rub my face, seeing Melanie outside the garage through the cracks in my fingers.

She carries a steaming bowl prepared in the camper. "You look like you need it," she says. I thank her for the chicken noodle soup, kiss her on the cheek and take it inside the zoom boom to eat.

As the broth slowly warms my body, I gaze around the community, past Mark, my neighbour, raking rocks outside his new shop, the fresh frames of Pam's house, and beyond the skeletons of seven charred vehicles on Stan's property, a car collection turned junkyard.

My eyes hold on white hills, looking vast and sturdy as ever with the forest thinned out.

Any insects or diseases that once thrived in the woods were killed by the flames, and the forest floor was cleaned of underbrush and invasive weeds. Soon, the snow will melt and open the earth to the brightest sunlight the hills have seen in hundreds of years. Wildflowers will bloom, and birds and mammals will return to graze on them. The soil will be nourished with nitrogen, absorbed from the decaying debris, allowing another generation of trees to grow stronger and healthier than the ones before. Life in Fort McMurray will carry on. Homes will be rebuilt, people will return, and lives will start over. What was once home will always be home.

ACKNOWLEDGEMENTS

Damian Asher: I thank my wife, Melanie, and kids, Aidan and Taya, for their love and support. Even after the loss of our house and possessions, Melanie still stands beside me and supports me through all my endeavours in life. This has been a difficult project for me, and without her beside me, I would not have been able to complete it. I love you.

As I am a firefighter and not a writer, I have to applaud Omar Mouallem for all his support and vigilance in writing this story with me. He has endured my long hours and my crazy life of family, work and house-building.

FMFD, your comradeship and brotherhood is relentless. Thanks for your stories and support. I can only hope that we've painted a good picture of the sacrifices some of you had to make. As I was born and raised in Fort McMurray, I thank you for everything you did and continue to do for our community.

Fort McMurray, I'm sorry for everything that has happened and everything you have had to go through, but I thank you for allowing us to serve you and keep you safe in your times of need. We will stand tall by you, always.

Omar Mouallem: I offer my deepest gratitude to my coauthor, Damian Asher, for inviting me into his unique world and sharing his incredible story. His stamina and loyalty are truly unmatched and still boggle my mind, even after exploring their depths. This book wouldn't have been possible without the participation of several other Fort McMurrayites and firefighters whose extensive interviews (and cellphone videos and photos) allowed us to piece together the whirlwind week of May 2, including Melanie, Peggy, Aidan and Taya Asher, Tia and Steve Morari, Mike Woykin, Matthew Heikel, Ryan Pitchers, Chris Relph, Joe Jamieson, Kyle Hitchcock, Trevor Shantz, Nathan Cseke, Adam Bugden, Nick Waddington, Chad Morrison, Michael Powlesland and Robin Smith.

Many thanks to my editor, Brendan May, and my agent, Jackie Kaiser, for midwifing *Inside the Inferno* within such an intense turnaround; this book was a huge undertaking for me, unlike anything I've done before, but with your assurances it was never too daunting. The editors of *SHARP* magazine, Greg Hudson and Peter Saltsman, who assigned the article that grew into this project, and photographers Aaron Pedersen and Mike Kuby, my partners in crime, deserve props too.

Lastly, I must thank my wife, Janae Jamieson, for being my first reader and occasional research assistant, my friend Curtis Gillespie, for teaching me the literary nonfiction craft some years ago, and other writerly friends for supporting me during this process in more mysterious ways: Marcello di Cintio, Jason Markusoff, Jennifer Cockrall-King and Michael Hingston.